ITALIAN GRAMMAR

ITALIAN GRAMMAR

Second Edition

By Lawrence Klibbe

Revised by Wayne Storey

University of Virginia

BARNES & NOBLE BOOKS
A DIVISION OF HARPER & ROW, PUBLISHERS
New York, Cambridge, Philadelphia,
San Francisco, London, Mexico City,
São Paulo, Sydney

Designer: C. Linda Dingler

Library of Congress Cataloging in Publication Data

Klibbe, Lawrence Hadfield, 1923–
  Italian grammar.

  English and Italian.
  Includes index.
  1. Italian language—Grammar—1950–   I. Storey, Wayne. II. Title.
PC1112.K5 1982   458.2'421   81–48165
ISBN 0–06–460199–4 (pbk.)   AACR2

82 83 84 85 86 10 9 8 7 6 5 4 3 2 1

CONTENTS

V

SUGGESTIONS

These suggestions are directed primarily to the student using *Italian Grammar* as a supplementary outline of essential grammatical points to improve his or her mastery of the language. However, this brief and summarizing treatment of Italian is designed also for those who have never studied the language before and wish a rapid course in essential Italian grammar. Following such a course, some basic considerations should be kept in mind.

1. ENGLISH GRAMMAR. This will normally *not* be stressed unless to clarify and emphasize a major difference between the English and Italian forms. Rather, it is suggested that the student concentrate on the Italian model and rely on memorization of clear and basic formulas, reducing the act of translating word for word to that of comprehending phrase patterns.

2. VOCABULARY. Here the main aim has been to employ a basic and essential vocabulary in all examples so that the student may have at his or her disposal the foundation for reading and speaking immediately. Further improvement in vocabulary should come from readers and other outside material.

3. VERBS AND THEIR USES. There is no doubt that the old dictum that verbs are the heart of a language is correct. Time and attention have been spent on stressing the verb in tenses, moods, and voices. Particular attention should be devoted to the distinctions in tense usage (particularly in the past tenses) with respect to related and sometimes confusing tenses: for example, the expressive potential of the present perfect, the imperfect, and the preterit.

4. STRUCTURE AND PHRASEOLOGY. The greatest differences between English and Italian are found in the arrangement and modification of words and phrases. What may be the most unlikely combination and order of words to a native speaker of English may for the Italian speaker be the most succinct expression of the simplest phenomenon, and vice versa. This often "idiomatic" structure reflects not only a different linguistic history and separate cultural development, but also a unique and equally concise means of perceiving and expressing the same event. These differences should be noted and given extra attention to facilitate a better understanding of the grammatical structure as well as the cultural basis of the language.

Chapters in this book vary in length and in difficulty. Review exercises test the student on the area covered by groupings of chapters. It is hoped that this grammar review will reinforce and clarify the student's comprehension of the Italian language for his or her own better knowledge and perhaps for a better mark on the next test.

GUIDE TO PRONUNCIATION: THE ALPHABET, VOWELS AND CONSONANTS, DOUBLE CONSONANTS, DIPHTHONGS, SYLLABLES, STRESS AND ACCENTS; CAPITALIZATION

THE ALPHABET

Letter	Name	Letter	Name
a	a	n	enne
b	bi	o	o
c	ci	p	pi
d	di	q	cu
e	e	r	erre
f	effe	s	esse
g	gi	t	ti
h	acca	u	u
i	i	v	vu
l	elle	z	zeta
m	emme		

These letters may be used in words of foreign derivation:

Letter	Name	Letter	Name
j	i lungo	x	ics
k	kappa	y	ipsilon
w	doppio vu		

Although English equivalents are listed for the corresponding sounds in Italian, the student should remember that these are only approximations.

VOWELS

a is pronounced like *a* in *father:* **sala.**
e (open) is pronounced like *e* in *set:* **contento, mensa.**

e (close) is pronounced like *a* in *baby:* **che, sera.**
i is pronounced like *i* in *machine:* **aprire.**
o (open) is pronounced like *o* in *off:* **porta, bocca.**
o (close) is pronounced like *o* in *open:* **pacco, posta.**
u is pronounced like *oo* in *cool:* **luna.**

Consonants

The consonants in Italian are pronounced approximately as the same consonants in English, but the following exceptions should be noted:

c is pronounced like *k* in *kitchen* before *a, o, u:* **casa.**
ch is also pronounced like *k* in *kitchen:* **chiesa.**
c is pronounced like *ch* in *church* before *e, i:* **cento.**
g is pronounced like *g* in *goat* before *a, o, u:* **gatto, gomma, guerra.**
g is pronounced like *g* in *general* before *e, i:* **gente, gioco.**
gh is pronounced like *g* in *get:* **laghi.**
gli may be difficult to master, but can be practiced through the rapid pronunciation of stee*ly*ard and the resulting *l* from the combination of the *ly:* **figlio, migliore.**
gn is pronounced like *ni* in *onion:* **sogno.**
h is *always* silent—*never* pronounce this letter.
qu is pronounced like *qu* in *question:* **quaderno.**
r is rolled, while the double *r* is trilled.
s is pronounced like *s* in *rose* before a voiced consonant (*b, d, g, l, m, n, r, v*) and between vowels: **sbaglio, slancio, mese.**
s is pronounced like *s* in *sent* at the beginning of a word before a vowel, when the *s* is doubled, and when the *s* is followed by a voiceless consonant (*c, f, p, q, t*): **subito, basso, spazio.**
z is pronounced like *ts* in *gets* in words such as: **zio, zucchero, pezzo.**
z is pronounced like *ds* in *pads* in words such as: **mezzo, pranzo, analizzare.**

Double Consonants

In Italian, all double consonants are pronounced, often distinguishing meaning. Some examples are: **sette, sete, sonno, sono, carro, caro.**

set-te	**seven**	sete	**thirst**
son-no	**sleep**	so-no	**I am, they are**
car-ro	**cart**	caro	**dear**

Some are only lengthened:

pazzo   faccia

Diphthongs

DEFINITION. Letters *a, e, o* are the strong vowels; *u* and *i* are the weak vowels. A combination of two vowels, weak and/or strong, forms a *diphthong*. The general principle for stress is:

1. FIRST VOWEL for these groups: *au, eu, ai, ei, oi, ui.*

2. SECOND VOWEL for these groups: *ie, io, ia, iu, ue, uo, ui.*

Syllables

Words are separated into syllables in this way:
1. *Single* consonants go with the *next* syllable: **sa-lu-to.**
2. A *double* consonant is separated: **bel-lo.**
3. If the *first* of two consonants is l, m, n, r, the syllable is divided: **bal-co-ne.**
4. Any other group of *two* consonants is pronounced with the *next* syllable: **fi-glio.**
5. Except for *s,* the *first* of three consonants will go with the preceding syllable: **al-tro, fi-ne-stra.**
6. A *diphthong* is *not* separated: **buo-no.**

Stress and Accents

1. In most Italian words the stress falls on the next-to-last (penultimate) syllable: **lavoro, contento, finestra.**

2. In some words the stress falls on the last syllable; this is always indicated in printed and written Italian by a grave accent: **città, università.**

3. In some words the stress falls on a syllable other than the next-to-last or the last; in this book such a stressed syllable will be indicated by a dot under the syllable's vowel: **subito, dialogo, abitano.**

CAPITALIZATION

Capitalization is used *less* in Italian than in English. Words in the following categories are *not* capitalized in Italian:

1. Days of the week.
2. Months of the year.
3. Proper adjectives. For example:
   Un libro *italiano*
   Giovanni è *italiano*
   BUT
   Gl'Italiani sono simpatici
4. Titles, including *Mr., Mrs., Miss*. For example:
   La *signora* Falcone
   Il *principe* Salerno
5. The pronoun for *I:* **io.**

Still capitalized in more conservative and formal situations, the following are now often written lower-case:
   she: ella
   you: lei (singular, polite)
   you: loro (plural, polite)

GENDER; SINGULAR AND PLURAL OF NOUNS; INDEFINITE AND DEFINITE ARTICLES

GENDER

All nouns are *masculine* or *feminine*. There is no neuter gender in Italian.

1. THE FIRST RULE is that of "natural" gender, implied in the meaning of the word:

uomo *man*	padre *father*	(masculine)
donna *woman*	sorella *sister*	(feminine)

2. THE ENDING of a noun will *generally* indicate the gender.

(a) If the noun ends in **o**, it is normally masculine.

(b) If the noun ends in **a**, it is normally feminine.

(c) If the noun ends in **e**, it may be either masculine or feminine and must be memorized for the proper gender:

Libro (masculine)

Scuola (feminine)

Esame (masculine)

Classe (feminine)

3. EXCEPTIONS. There are some exceptions to these rules which must be learned. For example, **mano** is feminine and **poeta** is masculine.

SINGULAR AND PLURAL OF NOUNS

The basic rule to follow initially is:

1. If the final letter of a singular noun is *o,* or *e,* change that letter to *i.*

2. If the final letter of a singular noun is *a,* change that letter to *e.*

Singular	Plural
libro	libri
professore	professori
scuola	scuole

EXCEPTIONS. Certain exceptions to the preceding rules occur in the irregular or orthographic formation of the noun.

1. Some masculine nouns which end in *o* in the singular change in the plural to feminine gender.

> uovo—uova   braccio—braccia   paio—paia

2. Generally, nouns ending in *co* and *go* and whose stress is penultimate change to *chi* and *ghi* in the plural, but some such nouns may form their plurals regularly.

> *fuoco* becomes *fuochi*
> *lago* becomes *laghi*
> *amico* becomes *amici*
> *mẹdico* becomes *mẹdici*

3. If a noun ends in *io:*
   (a) *io* becomes *ii* if the singular *i* is stressed.

> *zio—zii*

   (b) *io* becomes *i* if the singular *i* is unstressed.

> *figlio—figli*

4. If a noun ends in *ca* or *ga*, the letter *h* is placed before the plural *e*.

> *amica* becomes *amiche*

5. If a noun *ends* with a written accent, no change is made for the plural.

> *università* (singular) remains *università* (plural).

In addition to these exceptions, other irregular formations may occur and must be learned by simple memorization. For example, **uomo** (singular) becomes **uọmini** (plural). When in doubt as to a noun's gender and plural form, consult the vocabulary for each lesson, the general vocabularies at the end of this book, or a good dictionary that gives such information. In most cases, however, Italian nouns follow the basic rules outlined here.

INDEFINITE ARTICLES

1. THE RULE. The indefinite articles (*a* and *an*) in Italian are:
(a) **Un** before a masculine noun.
   un muro
(b) **Una** before a feminine noun.
   una casa

2. EXCEPTIONS:

(a) **Uno** before masculine nouns beginning with *z* or "impure *s*" (*s* + a consonant).

uno zọccolo

uno stato

(b) Note that before a *feminine noun* that begins with a vowel, **una** becomes *un'*.

un'isola   un'amica

3. THERE IS NO PLURAL for the indefinite article. The use of *di* + the definite article for expressing "some" and "any" will be treated later.

DEFINITE ARTICLES

The definite article (*the*) in Italian must agree in gender and number with the noun to which it belongs. The definite article normally precedes the noun.

1. MASCULINE. For the masculine gender, two basic singular forms are used:

(a) **il** before nouns beginning with a consonant, forming its plural in *i*.

il libro   i libri   il cane   i cani

(b) **lo** before nouns beginning with a vowel, an "impure *s*" or a *z*. It forms its plural in **gli.**

l'invitato*—gl'invitati*

lo sbaglio—gli sbagli

lo zio—gli zii

*Note that *lo* before a vowel becomes *l'*, while *gli* before an *i* elides to *gl'* (**gl'Italiani,** but **gli Americani**).

2. FEMININE. For the feminine gender, one set of articles (singular and plural) is used.

(a) *La* (singular) and *le* (plural).

la stazione   *le* stazioni

(b) **La** before a noun beginning with a vowel becomes *l'*.

l'epoca   l'amica

3. USAGE. Unlike English, the indefinite and definite articles are usually repeated before each noun.

The men and women   Gli uọmini e le donne

A hat and coat   Un cappello e un cappotto

The following chart will aid in the memorization of the forms of the definite articles.

	Masculine	Feminine
Singular	il lo l'	la l'
Plural	i gli gli	le le

OBSERVATIONS

1. The main idea to bear in mind is that the indefinite or the definite article must agree in gender and number with the noun it modifies. For example, if a noun is feminine plural (**stagioni**), the article must be feminine plural (**le stagioni**).

2. The student will find it most helpful to (a) learn carefully the *gender* and *ending* of each noun (noting especially irregular plurals) as s/he encounters a new word, and (b) maintain a personal continuing vocabulary list of problematic or hard-to-remember nouns which may turn up repeatedly in readings.

SUBJECT PRONOUNS; MOOD AND THE PRESENT INDICATIVE TENSE; MOST COMMON IRREGULAR VERBS

SUBJECT PRONOUNS

The subject pronouns in Italian are:

	Singular		Plural	
1st person:	**io**	I	**noi**	we
2nd person:	**tu**	you	**voi**	you
3rd person:	**lui**	he	**loro**	they (m.)
	lei	she	**loro**	they (f.)
	Lei	you	**Loro**	you

The above forms of the subject pronouns are the ones used increasingly in the spoken language, but other forms may be encountered in reading, writing, and formal conversation.

	Singular		Plural	
3rd person:	**egli**	he	**essi**	they (m.)
	ella	she	**esse**	they (f.)
	esso	it (m.)		
	essa	it (f.)		

Subject pronouns are usually not expressed in Italian because the ending of a verb will indicate the person and the number. However, subject pronouns are used for emphasis, clarity, and contrast. If a sentence contains any of these elements, then the subject pronoun is inserted.

THE POLITE AND FAMILIAR. The rendering of the "you" address in Italian may cause some confusion for the beginning student. Note that there is a socio-grammatical division between the *polite* (**Lei**) and the *familiar* (**tu**) forms of address.

Use the following rules regarding the *polite* form:

(a) **Lei** is used for "you" singular when addresssing a person toward whom a certain respect is expected or desired, including mutual respect or a difference in social level (as with a doctor, a lawyer, a teacher, an older person, or even a new acquaintance). The accompanying verb must be third person singular.

Viene, Lei? *Are your coming, Sir?*

(b) **Loro** is used for the plural address, using third person plural.

Vengono, Loro? *Are you coming (ladies and gentlemen)?*

Use the following guidelines regarding the *familiar* form:

(a) **Tu** (singular) is used usually with: (1) members of the family, (2) close friends—people with whom you are on a first-name basis, (3) children, and (4) animals. The accompanying form of the verb must be second person singular.

Vieni tu? *Are you coming?*

(b) **Voi** is used for plural address, now in use also for groups of people who may be addressed individually with the **Lei** form. In today's usage **Loro** (polite plural) is required only in the most formal situations. For **voi** the accompanying form of the verb must be second person plural.

Venite voi? *Are you coming?*

Note that in the past the polite forms were much more widely used. But today the strictness of the polite forms is giving way to less formal speech, particularly in egalitarian settings. Nevertheless, it is important for the student to be competent in both forms of address, and close attention should be given to both.

Note: **Ciao** (used for both "hello" and "goodbye") is used only with people whom you would address as *tu*.

Mood

A mood is a form of a verb which explains the way in which a state or action is to be expressed. Like English, Italian has three separate categories of moods: 1. To make a statement or ask a question. 2. To convey doubt, uncertainty, contrary-to-fact expressions, wishes, and certain idiomatic constructions. 3. To give a command or make a request.

The first is the *indicative* mood; the second is the *subjunctive* mood; the third is the *imperative* mood. These three moods will be taken up in this order, beginning with the *present tense* of the *indicative*.

PRESENT TENSE

The point of departure for all verbs in Italian is the infinitive. This is the form which is listed first in vocabularies and dictionaries. Thus, if you wish to know the word for "speak" or "talk" in Italian, you will find the form **parlare,** which means "to speak" or "to talk."

There are three conjugations of verbs in Italian. (The third will be discussed in Topic 5.) These classes of verbs are determined by the ending of the verb.

1. If an infinitive ends in *-are,* then the verb belongs to the *first* conjugation.

   parlare—first conjugation

2. If an infinitive ends in *-ere,* then the verb belongs to the *second* conjugation.

   vendere—second conjugation

In each of the two examples, the infinitive may be divided into the "root," or the "stem," as the first part, and the "ending" as the second part.

parlare	*parl-*	root or stem
	-are	ending
vendere	*vend-*	root or stem
	-ere	ending

It is important to keep this distinction in mind because the formation of the *tenses* in Italian will be based upon the root or stem of the verb.

The present tense in Italian is formed by dropping the *ending* of the infinitive and inserting a new set of endings.

1. To the root of an *-are* infinitive, such as **parlare,** these endings are added:

	Singular	*Plural*
1st person:	**-o**	**-iamo**
2nd person:	**-i**	**-iate**
3rd person:	**-a**	**-ano**

2. To the root of an *-ere* infinitive, such as **vendere,** these endings are added:

	Singular	*Plural*
1st person:	-o	-iamo
2nd person:	-i	-ete
3rd person:	-e	-ono

3. Thus, the present tenses of the verbs **parlare** and **vendere** are formed as follows:

	Singular	*Plural*
1st person:	**parlo**	**parliamo**
2nd person:	**parli**	**parlate**
3rd person:	**parla**	**parlano**
1st person:	**vendo**	**vendiamo**
2nd person:	**vendi**	**vendete**
3rd person:	**vende**	**vendono**

One should always look for similarities in the endings of the various tenses. For example, the endings of the first and second persons singular and the first person plural are the same in the present tense in both conjugations. And only the first vowel of the ending undergoes any change in the other three persons of the first and second conjugations.

TEMPORAL DISTINCTIONS of the present tense. The present tense in Italian has *three* possible renditions in English.

1. **Parlo** and **vendo** may express three separate states in the present:
   parlo *I speak, I do speak, I am speaking*
   vendo *I sell, I do sell, I am selling*

2. In English, these variations of the present tense may be considered as the simple present, the emphatic present, and the progressive tenses.

3. Since the three forms of the present tense are expressed by the same verbal form in Italian, auxiliary words (such as "do," "am," and "are") are *not* stated.

Therefore, the expression of the present tense in Italian, using the *regular* verbs **parlare** and **vendere** as examples, with the subject pronouns (understood but *not* stated), and with the corresponding English translations, will be as follows:

parlare—to speak

(io)   parlo   *I speak, I do speak, I am speaking*

(tu)	parli	*you speak, you do speak, you are speaking*
(egli, ella lui, lei)	parla	*he, she, it speaks; he, she, it does speak; he, she, it is speaking*
(Lei)	parla	*you speak, you do speak, you are speaking*
(noi)	parliamo	*we speak, we do speak, we are speaking*
(voi)	parlate	*you speak, you do speak, you are speaking*
(loro, essi, esse)	pạrlano	*they speak, they do speak, they are speaking*
(Loro)	pạrlano	*you speak, you do speak, you are speaking*

vẹndere—to sell

(io)	vendo	*I sell, I do sell, I am selling*
(tu)	vendi	*you sell, you do sell, you are selling*
(egli, ella, lui, lei)	vende	*he, she, it sells; he, she, it does sell; he, she, it is selling*
(Lei)	vende	*you sell, you do sell, you are selling*
(noi)	vendiamo	*we sell, we do sell, we are selling*
(voi)	vendete	*you sell, you do sell, you are selling*
(loro, essi, esse)	vẹndono	*they sell, they do sell, they are selling*
(Loro)	vẹndono	*you sell, you do sell, you are selling*

From this point on, the tenses in Italian will be developed according to this model. The subject pronouns will not be indicated in succeeding lessons. Therefore, the preceding detailed outline of the present tense for the first and second conjugations should be referred to by the reader. **Parlare** and **vẹndere** are regular verbs of the first and second conjugations. Their endings follow a certain pattern; if one learns the proper set of endings, then all regular verbs can be conjugated in the same fashion.

MOST COMMON IRREGULAR VERBS

Unfortunately, some verbs do not adhere to any established set of rules. These are irregular verbs which must be memorized as they occur. While the majority of verbs in Italian fall within the catego-

ry of regular verbs of the three conjugations, some verbs of high
frequency are irregular verbs.

Four of the most common irregular verbs are:

avere	*to have*
ęssere	*to be*
stare	*to be*
fare	*to do, to make*

Avere and **ęssere** are auxiliary verbs used to construct the compound tenses in Italian. (For example, **ho** visto, **sono** andato.) For
this reason, pay close attention to these two verbs.

Ęssere and **stare** often appear to mean the same thing in English.
They both express the concept "to be." However, in Italian their
uses and meanings are different and distinct. These differences in
meaning will be covered later.

The forms of these basic verbs should be memorized.

Present Tense

avere	ho	abbiamo
	hai	avete
	ha	hanno
ęssere	sono	siamo
	sei	siete
	è	sono
stare	sto	stiamo
	stai	state
	sta	stanno
fare	faccio (fo)	facciamo
	fai	fate
	fa	fanno

Note: This procedure also illustrates the pattern to be followed in
this book for the tenses of all verbs.

Other commonly used irregular verbs should be learned immediately in the *present tense.* Consult the list of irregular verbs at the end
of this book.

andare *to go* (p. 121)
bere *to drink* (p. 121)

dire *to say* (p. 122)

sapere *to know, to know how to*

Here are some examples, used in sentences:

1. Lui *va* a casa e io *vado* in biblioteca.
   He is going home and I am going to the library.

2. *Bevo* il vino di Roma.
   I'm drinking Roman wine.

3. *Dico* ciò che penso.
   I say what I think.

4. Loro *sanno* ciò che diciamo.
   They know what we are saying.
   Lei *sa* suonare il pianoforte.
   She knows how to play the piano.

THE THIRD CONJUGATION; SENTENCE PATTERNS; IDIOMATIC USAGE; DEFINITE AND INDEFINITE ARTICLES—FURTHER USES

THE THIRD CONJUGATION

In Topic 4, the conjugations for *-are* and *-ere* verbs were discussed. The third grouping consists of all verbs whose infinitives end in *-ire*.

To the root of an *-ire* infinitive, such as **partire,** these endings are added:

	Singular	Plural
1st person:	o	iamo
2nd person:	i	ite
3rd person:	e	ono

Thus, the present tense of the verb **partire** is formed as follows:

	Singular	Plural
1st person:	parto	partiamo
2nd person:	parti	partite
3rd person:	parte	partono

However, many Italian verbs ending in *-ire* require the insertion of *-isc* as part of the endings in all persons in the singular and in the third person plural. Thus, for **capire** (to understand), the conjugation is as follows:

Singular		Plural	
(io)	cap-isc-*o*	(noi)	cap-*iamo*
(tu)	cap-isc-*i*	(voi)	cap-*ite*
(lei/lui)	cap-isc-*e*	(loro)	cap-isc-*ono*

Note the similarities and differences in the endings of the three conjugations:

	-are	*-ere*	*-ire*	OR
(io)	-o	-o	-o	-isc*o*
(tu)	-i	-i	-i	-isc*i*
(lei/lui)	-*a*	-e	-e	-isc*e*
(noi)	-iamo	-iamo	-iamo	-iamo
(voi)	-*a*te	-*e*te	-*i*te	-*i*te
(loro)	-ano	-ono	-ono	-ịsc*ono*

From this table, it is easy to see that first and second person singular always end in *o* and *i,* respectively. Third person singular has but one variation: *a/e,* like third person plural *-ano/ono.* First person plural is always *-iamo.* Second person plural is formed with the first vowel of the infinitive ending plus *te:* for example, port-*are* is port -*a*te, fin-ire is fin -*i*te.

The difficulty in determining which *-ire* verbs require the *-isc* form will decrease with familiarity and practice. If in doubt, always consult a dictionary or check this book's Vocabulary, in which *-ire* verbs that take *-isc* are marked with a plus (+).

SENTENCE PATTERNS

The four principal types of sentence patterns are now apparent: the *declarative,* the *interrogative,* the *negative,* and the *negative–interrogative.*

1. *declarative:* Il padre arriva presto.
The father is arriving soon.

2. *interrogative:* Arriva presto il padre?
Is the father arriving soon?

3. *negative:* Il padre non arriva presto.
The father is not arriving soon.

4. *negative-interrogative:* Non arriva presto il padre?
Isn't the father arriving soon?

INTERROGATIVE SENTENCES are easy to form. These are sentences that ask a question. They may be done in several ways.

1. INVERSION of the word order of a statement. This may include the placement of the subject at the end of the question, as with the third example below.

Marco studia la lezione. *Marco is studying the lesson.*
Studia Marco la lezione? *Is Marco studying the lesson?*
Studia la lezione Marco? *Is Marco studying the lesson?*

2. INFLECTION of the declarative statement, adding the question mark.

Marco fa i compiti stasera?
Is Marco doing his homework tonight?
Note the declarative form: **Marco fa i compiti stasera.**

3. ADDITION of **non è vero?** or **vero?**

Marco studia la lezione, non è vero? *Marco is studying the lesson, isn't he?*

Marco fa i compiti stasera, vero? *Marco is doing his homework tonight, isn't he?*
Note the simplification of the usually difficult addition in English of "isn't he" or "doesn't he," rendered by the **non è vero?** (is that not true?) or **vero?** (true?) construction in Italian.

NEGATIVE SENTENCES AND THE DOUBLE NEGATIVE. A negative sentence is formed by placing the word **non** before the verb.

Gli studenti non capiscono il professore. *The students don't understand the professor.*
Italian usually depends upon the double negative (**non** + another negative expression)—a form not acceptable in standard English—to express the following negatives:

non . . . mai (never)	Non dorme mai. *He never sleeps.*
non . . . niente (nothing)	Non vende niente. *She's not selling anything.*
non . . . nulla (nothing)	Non faccio nulla. *I'm not doing anything.*
non . . . nessuno (no one)	Non vedo nessuno. *I don't see anyone.*
non . . . nè . . . nè (Neither . . . nor)	Non fa nè caldo nè freddo. *It's neither hot nor cold.*
neanche (not even)	Neanche lui capisce tutto. *Not even he understands everything.*
non . . . più (no more, no longer)	Non aspettiamo più il dentista. *We're not waiting (we won't wait) any longer for the dentist.*

IDIOMATIC USE OF THE PRESENT TENSE

If an action begins in the past and continues into the present, the present indicative form of the verb is used.

Studiamo l'italiano da due anni. *We have been studying Italian for two years.*

Notice the tense change in English!

In the above example, the use of the present tense in Italian indicates that the subject *still* studies Italian. Whereas:

Ho studiato l'italiano per due anni. *I studied Italian for two years.*

tells us that the subject no longer studies the language; that is,

Non studio più l'italiano. *I no longer study Italian.*

DEFINITE AND INDEFINITE ARTICLES—FURTHER USES

1. CONCEPTS. The definite article is used with nouns that express a *general* idea or an *abstract* concept.

Il tempo è prezioso. *Time is precious.*

La sincerità è una virtù. *Sincerity is a virtue.*

2. TITLES. The definite article is used with *titles* **except** in *direct address.*

Il professore viene ora. *The professor is coming now.*

Come sta, Signorina Sallese? *How are you, Miss Sallese?*

3. GEOGRAPHICAL NAMES. The definite article is used with the name of a large geographical unit, such as a country or large island.

L'Italia è in Europa. *Italy is in Europe.*

La Sicilia è bella. *Sicily is beautiful.*

Exception. The definite article is **omitted** when the preposition *in* (to, in) is used before a geographical name that is feminine and unmodified. Otherwise, the definite article is retained.

La città è negli Stati Uniti. *The city is in the United States.*

Stati Uniti is masculine plural.

BUT

Roma è **in** Italia. *Rome is in Italy.*

AND

Vado **in** Francia. *I'm going to France.*

BUT

Vado *nella* bella Francia. *I'm going to beautiful France.*

Exception. The indefinite article is **omitted** with an *unmodified* predicate noun indicating a profession, religion, or nationality.

Giuseppe è studente. *Joseph is a student.*

BUT

Giuseppe è un buono studente. *Joseph is a good student.*

THE ADJECTIVE: POSITION AND FORM; IRREGULAR PLURALS

Since an adjective is used to modify a noun, the rules for the formation of the singular and plural, masculine and feminine forms generally follow those established for nouns. Adjectives, like nouns, are divided into two basic *declensions,* or groups of endings. The following show the first and second declensions:

1. FIRST DECLENSION

	Singular	Plural
masculine	-o (italiano)	-i (italiani)
feminine	-a (italiana)	-e (italiane)

2. SECOND DECLENSION

	Singular	Plural
masculine and feminine	-e (francese)	-i (francesi)

Notice that in the second declension, masculine and feminine singular adjectives have the same endings, as do masculine and feminine plural adjectives.

il libro italiano—i libri italiani
la rivista italiana—le riviste italiane
il libro francese—i libri francesi
la rivista francese—le riviste francesi

An adjective must agree in number and gender with the noun it modifies. Don't be fooled by seemingly dissimilar endings: for example, le città francesi is the correct rendering for "the French cities."

POSITION AND FORM

An adjective either describes or limits (in the sense of "specifies") the noun it modifies. The following general rules can be applied:

1. *Descriptive* adjectives go *after* the modified noun.
2. *Limiting* adjectives go *before* the modified noun.

DESCRIPTIVE ADJECTIVES. These normally *follow* the noun. However, some exceptions to this rule are:

antico	*ancient, old*	giovane	*young*
bello	*beautiful*	grande	*big, great, large*
bravo	*fine, able*	lungo	*long*
breve	*brief, short*	nuovo	*new*
brutto	*mean, ugly*	piccolo	*little, small*
buono	*good*	stesso	*same*
cattivo	*bad*		

If one wishes to emphasize the quality, then even these adjectives come after the noun. This is a matter of style and depends a great deal upon the speaker's intention.

(a) Some adjectives may change meaning, depending upon their position *before* or *after* the noun.

Il professore povero. *The poor professor.* (in terms of money)

Il povero professore. *The poor professor.* (unfortunate)

(b) Note that adjectives of: (1) race, religion, nationality; (2) color; (3) shape; and (4) temperature always *follow* the noun.

(c) Some common descriptive adjectives which normally precede the noun have more inflected forms. Two such adjectives are **bello** and **buono**. The first follows the usage of the definite article to determine its forms, while the second is determined by the indefinite article usage.

For **bello**:

un bel libro (*il* libro)

un bel*lo* stato (*lo* stato)

un bel*l*'armadio (l'armadio)

For **buono** (remembering the indefinite articles):

un *buon* libro (*un* libro)

un buo*no* stato (*uno* stato)

un *buon* armadio (*un* armadio

For the plural forms of **bello**:

I libri sono *belli*

Sono *bei* libri

Le *belle* ragazze; Le ragazze sono *belle*

Note **belli** becomes **begli** (**begl'** before an *i*) before a vowel and the "s impure" combination.

LIMITING ADJECTIVES. The proper position of *limiting* adjectives is *before* the nouns they modify.

Two classifications of limiting adjectives are: the *demonstrative* and the *possessive* adjectives.

DEMONSTRATIVE ADJECTIVES. In English, the demonstrative adjectives are "this" and "that" in the singular; "these" and "those" in the plural. The corresponding forms in Italian are:

questo	*Singular*	*Plural*
masculine	questo	questi
feminine	questa	queste

Questo ragazzo e queste ragazze. *This boy and these girls.*

Note that **quest'** is used in the singular if the noun begins with a vowel; **quest'** is used in the plural if the noun begins with *e* or *i*.

quello	*Singular*	*Plural*
masculine	quello	quelli
feminine	quella	quelle

Quel ristorante e quelle case. *That restaurant and those houses.*

It is important to note that **questo** inflects like most adjectives, whereas **quello** resembles **bello** in its formation, cueing on the definite article pattern:

quel ragazzo	quei ragazzi
quello stato	quegli stati
quell'amico	quegli amici
quella ragazza	quelle ragazze
quell'amica	quelle amiche

POSSESSIVE ADJECTIVES. In English, the possessive adjective (*my, our, his,* etc.) agrees with the possessor. In Italian, the possessive adjective agrees with the thing possessed. Like all adjectives, the possessive adjective must be in agreement with the *noun modified*.

1. The forms are:

(a) *masculine*	*Singular*	*Plural*
	il mio	i miei
	il tuo	i tuoi

il suo	i suoi
il nostro	i nostri
il vostro	i vostri
il loro	i loro

(b) *feminine*   *Singular*   *Plural*

la mia	le mie
la tua	le tue
la sua	le sue
la nostra	le nostre
la vostra	le vostre
la loro	le loro

2. The order of a phrase with the possessive adjective will be: DEFINITE ARTICLE–POSSESSIVE ADJECTIVE–NOUN.

Il mio libro. *My book.*

La sua matita. *His (or her) pencil.*

3. The definite article is always used with the possessive adjective except in the following situations:

(a) Singular, unmodified kinship not using **loro**;

mio padre   sua sorella

il loro padre BUT *le* sue sorelle

(b) Some idiomatic uses and direct address:

Viene a casa mia. *He's coming to my house.*

Amico mio, come stai? *My friend, how are you?*

4. In the case of **suo, sua, suoi, sue,** context normally determines meaning (*his* or *her* or even *your*). However, to avoid ambiguity, **suo** and **suoi** and **sua** and **sue** may be replaced by **di lui** and **di lei.**

la sua matita   *his/her pencil*

la matita *di lui*   *his pencil*

la matita *di lei*   *her pencil*

INTERROGATIVE ADJECTIVES which agree with the noun are: **quanto, quanta, quanti, quante** (*how much, how many*); and **quale, quale, quali, quali** (*which*). Their established position is *before* the noun, so that these interrogative adjectives are also classified as limiting adjectives.

1. "What" as a limiting adjective is rendered as **che** in **che cosa;** however this phrase often becomes simply **che** or **cosa.**

Che cosa vuol dire? *What does that mean?*
Cosa fai? Che fai? *What are you doing?*
2. "Whose" as a limiting adjective is rendered as **di chi.**
 Di chi è questa lęttera? *Whose letter is this?*
 Questa lęttera è *di* lui. *This letter is his.*
*Notice the repetition of the preposition **di** in the response.

IRREGULAR PLURALS FOR ADJECTIVES

Some rules should be memorized to avoid confusion.
1. If a feminine adjective ends in *ca* or *ga,* then the letter *h* must be used in the plural: **lunga, lunghe.**
2. If a masculine adjective ends in *go,* then *h* is used in the plural: **lungo, lunghi.**
3. If a masculine adjective ends in *co* with the stress on the preceding syllable, the letter *h* is inserted in the plural: **bianco, bianchi.**
4. If a feminine adjective ends in *cia* or *gia,* then the *i* is omitted when the plural ending is added: **grigia, grige.**
The preceding rules also hold true for *nouns* which fall into those categories.

THE POSSESSIVE; THE PARTITIVE; PREPOSITIONS

THE POSSESSIVE

In English, possession may be indicated in two ways:
(a) By the use of the word "of" as part of the prepositional phrase.
The book of the boy
(b) By the use of "'s" in the singular and "s'" in the plural.
In Italian, the equivalents of the "'s" and "s'" do not exist, so that possession must be expressed by the prepositional phrase using the word *di* ("of"). With a vowel, *di* becomes *d'*.

Il libro di Roberto. *Robert's book.*

Il libro d'Antonio. *Antonio's book.*

THE "PREPOSIZIONI ARTICOLATE." When the preposition *di* occurs with the definite article singular and plural, the following "contractions" take place.

di and *il*	del
di and *lo*	dello
di and *la*	della
di and *i*	dei
di and *gli*	degli
di and *gl'*	degl'
di and *le*	delle

No: L'aula *di la* università.
Yes: L'aula *dell'*università.
  The university's room.
No: La penna *di la* ragazza.
Yes: La penna *della* ragazza.
  The girl's pen.

THE PARTITIVE

The idea of the *partitive* (*part* of the *whole* concept) is expressed in English by the words "some" or "any." In Italian, the words "some" or "any" are translated by the preposition **di** and the corresponding *definite* article.

Comprano del pane. *They are buying some bread.*

However, if the sentence is *negative* or *interrogative,* then the partitive is frequently *not* used.

Vende Lei libri? *Are you selling some books?*

Non vendo libri. *I am not selling any books.*

The following expressions are also considered as partitives: **alcuni, alcune, qualche, un po' di.**

PREPOSITIONS

In addition to the "contracting" of **di** plus the forms of the definite article, the following prepositions change when used with definite articles:

a	*a* and *il*	al	**da**	*da* and *il*	dal
	a and *lo*	allo		*da* and *lo*	dallo
	a and *la*	alla		*da* and *la*	dalla
	a and *l'*	all'		*da* and *l'*	dall'
	a and *i*	ai		*da* and *i*	dai
	a and *gli*	agli		*da* and *gli*	dagli
	a and *gl'*	agl'		*da* and *gl'*	dagl'
	a and *le*	alle		*da* and *le*	dalle
in	*in* and *le*	nel	**su**	*su* and *il*	sul
	in and *lo*	nello		*su* and *lo*	sullo
	in and *la*	nella		*su* and *la*	sulla
	in and *l'*	nell'		*su* and *l'*	sull'
	in and *i*	nei		*su* and *i*	sui
	in and *gli*	negli		*su* and *gli*	sugli
	in and *gl'*	negl'		*su* and *gl'*	sugl'
	in and *le*	nelle		*su* and *le*	sulle

Be careful not to assign any one meaning to the preposition in Italian. The following meanings are usually employed:

di *of, from* (This meaning has been seen in the use of **di** as
    meaning possession.)
a   *at, in, to*
da *by, from, at the house of, at the office of*
in *in, into, within*
su *on, upon*

But in a sentence their meanings may vary:
Vado *in* Amęrica. *I'm going to Amęrica.*
Sono *a* Firenze. *I'm in Florence.*
Finally, become familiar with the contracted forms of **con** ("with")
and **per** ("through," "in order to"), found normally in journalistic
prose.

$$con + il = col \qquad con + i = coi$$
$$per + il = pel \qquad per + i = pei$$

REVIEW EXERCISES, TOPICS 2–7

PATTERN DRILLS. Write the following sentences, changing the
verb to agree with the following subject pronouns: (1) noi; (2) loro;
(3) lei; (4) io; (5) voi; (6) tu.
1. Non parlo inglese.
2. Studio quelle lezioni a casa.
3. Ripeto le parole lunghe.
4. Ascolto ora.
5. Ho il libro di Marta.
6. Capisco molto bene.
7. Non sono in Italia, sono in Svizzera.
8. Vado a Firenze.
9. Non sapete niente.
10. Dico la verità.

TRANSLATE the following sentences into Italian.
1. John never reads the Italian lessons.
2. Good morning, Miss Bolaffi. How are you?
3. Are you going to the university today?
4. We are not studying Italian today or tomorrow.
5. He listens to the professor and he understands everything.
6. Why is she arriving early at school?
7. Mr. Buoncore is a good teacher.
8. You (pl.) are doing all the lessons, aren't you?

9. Are we leaving for Rome soon?
10. When does he get (arrive) home?
11. They prefer Joseph's automobile. It's very beautiful.
12. Here is the doctor! He's running.
13. You know everything.
14. Is he drinking the water?
15. We are going to the museum.

TRANSLATE the following sentences into Italian. Then wherever possible change all units to the plural.

1. The boy is finishing this book.
2. Does the girl understand those lessons?
3. The French city is beautiful.
4. He listens to the professor of Italian.
5. I am not at the university; it is she who goes (*frequentare*) to that university.
6. I'm going home to (in order to) do my homework.
7. His brother has my pencil.
8. He knows the homework.
9. We are going to Arezzo to see the churches.
10. They are making beautiful blue boxes.

GIVE the correct *preposizione articolata* (contracted preposition) before each noun.

1. (di) ____ scuola, ____ stato, ____ lezioni, ____ ragazzi, ____ amico
2. (su) ____ tavola, ____ giornale, ____ libri, ____ antico libro, ____ casa
3. (da) ____ padre, ____ stesso ragazzo, ____ scrittori, ____ vocabolario
4. (in) ____ libro, ____ piccola casa, ____ caso, ____ stati, ____ bagni
5. (a) ____ studenti, ____ amiche, ____ macchina, ____ telefono
6. (con) ____ ragazzo, ____ professore, ____ un buon libro, ____ automobile.

NUMBERS; DAYS, SEASONS, MONTHS; TELLING OF TIME; IRREGULAR VERBS IN THE PRESENT TENSE: TENERE, VENIRE, DARE

NUMBERS

THE CARDINAL NUMBERS. Note stress markings (*ųndici*) for some pronunciations.

0	zero	21	ventuno	60	sessanta
1	uno, una	22	ventidue	70	settanta
2	due	23	ventitrè	80	ottanta
3	tre	24	ventiquattro	90	novanta
4	quattro	25	venticinque	100	cento
5	cinque	26	ventisei	101	centouno
6	sei	27	ventisette	102	centodue
7	sette	28	ventotto	103	centotre
8	otto	29	ventinove	110	centodieci
9	nove	30	trenta	120	centoventi
10	dieci	31	trentuno	121	centoventuno
11	ųndici	32	trentadue	130	centotrenta
12	dọdici	33	trentatrè	140	centoquaranta
13	trẹdici	34	trentaquattro	200	duecento
14	quattọrdici	35	trentacinque	1.000	mille
15	quịndici	36	trentasei	1.500	millecinquecento
16	sẹdici	37	trentasette	2.000	duemila
17	diciassette	38	trentotto	2.500	duemilacinquecento
18	diciotto	39	trentanove	100.000	centomila
19	diciannove	40	quaranta	1.000.000	un milione
20	venti	50	cinquanta	2.000.000	due milioni

Points to remember:

1. The indefinite article in the singular is also used as the cardinal number one.

2. **Cento** means "one hundred"—the "one" in the group is *not* expressed.

3. The numbers **venti, trenta, quaranta, cinquanta, sessanta, settanta, ottanta,** and **novanta** do not use the last vowel when joined with **uno** and **otto.**

4. The number **tre** must be accented when expressing "twenty-three," "thirty-three," etc.

Il francobollo vale duemilatrecentoquaranta dollari.

The stamp is worth $2,340.

Note: In English one may say "twenty-three hundred and forty dollars," as well as "two thousand, three hundred and forty dollars"; in Italian, only the latter method of counting is used.

THE ORDINAL NUMBERS

1st	primo	14th	quattordicęsimo
2nd	secondo	15th	quindicęsimo
3rd	terzo	20th	ventęsimo
4th	quarto	21st	ventunęsimo
5th	quinto	22nd	ventiduęsimo
6th	sesto	23rd	ventitreęsimo
7th	sęttimo	30th	trentęsimo
8th	ottavo	100th	centęsimo
9th	nono	101th	centęsimo primo
10th	dęcimo	102nd	centęsimo secondo
11th	undicęsimo	2000th	duemillęsimo
12th	dodicęsimo	1000000th	milionęsimo
13th	tredicęsimo		

Note: The ordinal numbers through *tenth* have distinct forms from the cardinal numbers. However, the ordinal numbers beginning with *eleventh* are formed by eliminating the last vowel of the cardinal number before adding the suffix -*ęsimo*. (Exception: 23, 33, 43, etc., do not drop that last vowel.)

DESIGNATION OF CENTURIES. Although centuries are designated by the ordinal numbers, the following modern eras have their own characteristic designation:

il Duecento	*13th century*
il Trecento	*14th century*
il Quattrocento	*15th century*
il Cinquecento	*16th century*
il Seicento	*17th century*
il Settecento	*18th century*

l'Ottocento	*19th century*
il Novecento	*20th century*

Of course, the designation may also be made explicitly.

Il quarto secolo *the fourth century*

NUMBERS AS ADJECTIVES. The cardinal and ordinal numbers are considered as *limiting* adjectives and as a rule are placed before the noun.

Il dęcimo libro *the tenth book*

With sovereigns and others with such numerical designations, the ordinal number will be after the noun.

Pio nono *Pius IX*

NUMBERS AS DATES. Dates are translated as *day, month, year*. Except for the first day of the month, cardinal numbers are employed for the dates; in the case of the first day, the ordinal number **primo** is used.

Il quattro luglio millesettecentosettantasei *July 4, 1776*

Il primo gennaio millenovecentosessantasette *January 1, 1967*

The translations commonly used for dates are:

Quanti ne abbiamo oggi?	*What is today's date?*
Oggi ne abbiamo . . . , or Oggi è il . . .	*Today's date is . . .*

DAYS, SEASONS, MONTHS

DAYS OF THE WEEK

domęnica	*Sunday*
lunedì	*Monday*
martedì	*Tuesday*
mercoledì	*Wednesday*
giovedì	*Thursday*
venerdì	*Friday*
sąbato	*Saturday*

The days of the week are *not* capitalized. They are all masculine, with the definite article **il**, except for Sunday, which has the definite article **la.**

In English, the singular is used for one day; the plural for more than one day. But in Italian:

Mi diverto *la* domęnica. *I have a good time on Sundays.*

Mi diverto domenica. *I have a good time on Sunday.*
Note: Sometimes the idea of *next* and *last* may be contained in the
day *without* the definite article.

THE SEASONS

la primavera	*spring*	l'autunno	*autumn*
l'estate (f.)	*summer*	l'inverno	*winter*

MONTHS OF THE YEAR. The months of the year are all masculine.

gennaio	*January*	luglio	*July*
febbraio	*February*	agosto	*August*
marzo	*March*	settembre	*September*
aprile	*April*	ottobre	*October*
maggio	*May*	novembre	*November*
giugno	*June*	dicembre	*December*

HOLIDAYS. Some of the principal holidays are:

il Capodanno	*New Year's Day*
l'Epifania	*Epiphany*
le Ceneri	*Ash Wednesday*
il Venerdì Santo	*Good Friday*
la Pasqua	*Easter*
la vigilia di Natale	*Christmas Eve*
il Natale	*Christmas*

TELLING OF TIME

The idea of time is translated literally in Italian by the word for
"hour" or "hours." It is, of course, impossible to translate exactly
into English this concept as used in Italian. Thus, the expression:

What time is it?

is rendered as:

Che ora è? *What hour is it?*

OR

Che ore sono? *What hours are they?*

The answer then becomes singular for the first hour (one o'clock),
noon and midnight and plural for all succeeding hours. (The words
ora and **ore** are not expressed, but are understood within the frame-
work of the answer.)

È l'una.	*It is one o'clock.*
È mezzogiorno	*It is noon.*
Sono le due.	*It is two o'clock.*
Sono le tre.	*It is three o'clock.*

QUARTER HOURS. The quarter divisions of the hour are determined by the addition or subtraction of the fifteen-minute period from the hour.

Sono le due e un quarto. *It is a quarter after two,* OR, *It is 2:15.*

Sono le due e mezzo. *It is half-past two,* OR, *It is 2:30.*

Sono le tre meno un quarto. *It is a quarter to three,* OR, *It is 2:45.*

Sono le tre meno venti minuti. *It is twenty minutes to three,* OR, *It is 2:40.*

COMMON EXPRESSIONS OF TIME

il mezzogiorno	*noon*
la mezzanotte	*midnight*
il giorno	*day*
il pomeriggio	*afternoon*
la notte	*night*
domani	*tomorrow*
oggi	*today*
ieri	*yesterday*
la mattina	*morning*
la sera	*evening*
in punto	*sharp, exactly*

Some other methods to express time in Italian are:

1. Official schedules use the twenty-four-hour system which, instead of stopping at noon and beginning the count again at one p.m., continues to twenty-four hours. Thus one p.m. is translated as "thirteen hours."

2. A.M. and P.M. are rendered as:

   (a) *di mattina*—in the morning, A.M.

   (b) *del pomeriggio*—in the afternoon, P.M.

   (c) *di sera*—in the evening, P.M.

3. Another way to tell time is by use of the verb **sonare.**

   Suona l'una. *It's striking one o'clock.*

   Suonano le due. *It's striking two o'clock.*

4. The verb **avere** is used to determine the age of a person. The English usage of "to be" is interpreted as "to have" in Italian.

Quanti anni ha Lei? OR Che età ha Lei? *How old are you?*

Ho quarantatrè anni. *I am forty-three years old.*

IRREGULAR VERBS IN THE PRESENT TENSE: TENERE, VENIRE, DARE.

Notice the similarities in the conjugation of **tenere** and **venire**. **Dare** is similar to an irregular already learned: **stare**.

tenere	teng*o*	ten*iamo*
	tien*i*	tèn*ete*
	tien*e*	tęng*ono*
venire	veng*o*	ven*iamo*
	vien*i*	ven*ite*
	vien*e*	vęng*ono*
dare	d*o*	d*iamo*
	da*i*	d*ate*
	d*à*	d*anno*

FUTURE AND CONDITIONAL TENSES; THE REFLEXIVE VERB; THE WEATHER; THE VERB "TO KNOW"; IRREGULAR FUTURE AND CONDITIONAL STEMS

THE FUTURE TENSE

The future tense is characterized by the use of "shall" and "will" in English. In Italian, the future tense is formed by using the *whole* infinitive, except for the final *e,* and adding the same set of endings for the three conjugations. However, in the first conjugation the ending yields *e* instead of *a;* and thus the future stem of **parlare** becomes **parler.** Some verbs such as **venire, andare,** and **fare** have irregular *future stems* and will be treated at the end of this chapter. The endings for the future tense are:

-ò	-emo
-ai	-ete
-à	-anno

Three model verbs in the future tense are conjugated as follows:

parlare	parlerò	parleremo
	parlerai	parlerete
	parlerà	parleranno
vendere	venderò	venderemo
	venderai	venderete
	vederà	venderanno
capire	capirò	capiremo
	capirai	capirete
	capirà	capiranno

OTHER USES. In addition to the regular use of the future tense to translate "shall" and "will," the following usages are observed:
1. Possibility and probability may be rendered by the future tense.

Daranno il romanzo al mędico. *They will probably give the novel to the doctor.*

2. If the future is understood in a dependent clause, then the future tense is used to express the dependent verb. (Both verbs are placed in the future tense.)

Quando verranno, partirò. *When they come, I shall leave.*

3. The concept of "going to" (showing intention) is sometimes expressed by the future.

Compreremo questa casa rossa. *We are going to buy this red house.* OR *We shall buy this red house.*

4. The present indicative may also be used if the action expressed is in the near future.

Mando il regalo a Giovanni. *I'm sending the gift to John.*

THE CONDITIONAL TENSE

The conditional tense should be compared with the future tense. Both tenses are formed in the same manner. For example, the conditional tense will also use the entire infinitive after omitting the final *e*; the same endings are added to the three conjugations; and the first conjugation will change the *a* in the stem to *e*. Note that the translation in English of the conditional tense is "should" or "would."

The endings for the conditional tense are:

-ei	-emmo
-esti	-este
-ebbe	-ębbero

Three model verbs in the conditional tense are conjugated as follows:

parlare	parlerei	parleremmo
	parleresti	parlereste
	parlerebbe	parlerębbero
vęndere	venderei	venderemmo
	venderesti	vendereste
	venderebbe	venderębbero
capire	capirei	capiremmo
	capiresti	capireste
	capirebbe	capirębbero

SPECIAL USES of the conditional tense are:

1. Possibility and probability in past time may be rendered by the conditional tense.

Ritornerębbero ben presto.

They were probably returning very soon.

2. Statements on the authority of someone else are placed in the conditional tense.

Secondo lui, starębbero a Roma.

According to him, they are in Rome.

3. The conditional tense must be used in the sequence of tenses with conditional sentences. This issue will be treated in Topic 17 under Conditional Sentences.

IRREGULAR FUTURE AND CONDITIONAL STEMS Some verbs have irregular stems to which the regular future and conditional endings are added. Of these irregulars there are three basic variations, typified by **venire, andare,** and **fare.**

1. Those verbs that undergo a complete change of the stem, containing a double *r*.

venire *verr*ò, *verr*ai, *verr*à, and so forth

tenere *terr*ò, *terr*ai, *terr*à, and so forth

2. Those verbs that drop an internal vowel.

Andare an*dr*ò, an*dr*ai, an*dr*à, and so forth

vedere ve*dr*ò, ve*dr*ai, ve*dr*à, and so forth

3. Those -*are* verbs that retain *a* in the future stem.

fare f*ar*ò, f*ar*ai, f*ar*à, and so forth

stare st*ar*ò, st*ar*ai, st*ar*à, and so forth

THE REFLEXIVE VERB

The reflexive verb is used more often in Italian than in English. In English the reflexive object, which "reflects" or refers back to the subject, is often understood. Thus "I am dressing" actually means "I am dressing *myself*." In Italian, the reflexive pronoun is always expressed.

The reflexive object must always agree with the subject; and there are reflexive objects corresponding to the subject for the three persons in the singular and in the plural, as follows:

io	mi	*myself*
tu	ti	*yourself* (informal)
lui ⎫		⎧ *himself*
lei ⎬ si		*herself*
Lei ⎭		⎩ *yourself* (formal)
noi	ci	*ourselves*
voi	vi	*yourselves* (informal)
loro ⎫ si		⎧ *themselves*
Loro ⎭		⎩ *yourselves* (formal)

A reflexive verb is indicated by the use of **si** attached to the infinitive; thus "to amuse oneself" is noted as **divertirsi (divertire + si)**

POSITION. Normally the reflexive object is before the verb. Thus the present tense of the reflexive verb **divertirsi** is:

mi diverto	ci divertiamo
ti diverti	vi divertite
si diverte	si divẹrtono

Shown in a sentence it is:

Io mi diverto. *I am having a good time.*

Io non m'alzo alle sette di mattina. *I do not get up at seven o'clock in the morning.*

USES. Some particular uses of the reflexive verb in addition to the regular usage are as follows:

1. The reflexive form may be employed to express the *reciprocal* idea.

Non si pạrlano. *They do not speak to each other.*

2. The indefinite person—"one," "you," "they," "people," etc.—is rendered by the reflexive form of the verb.

Si parla italiano. *People speak Italian.* OR *Italian is spoken.*

3. As observed in the preceding example, the reflexive form is one method of expressing the *passive voice* when the sentence includes no agent or doer of the action.

Si mạndano molte lẹttere. *Many letters are sent.*

4. The reflexive object may be used with the definite article before the noun when an article of clothing or a part of the body is involved.

Mi metto il cappello. *I put on my hat.*

Mi lavo le mani. *I wash my hands.*

THE WEATHER

An impersonal reaction to the weather will generally use the verb **fare.** A personal reaction to the weather will generally use the verb **avere.**

Che tempo fa? *How is the weather?*

Fa bel tempo. *The weather is beautiful.*

Ha freddo Lei? *Are you cold?*

Non ho freddo. *I am not cold.*

Fa freddo oggi. *It is cold today.*

Note these uses of **fare** and **avere** with the weather:

fare caldo OR avere caldo *to be warm*

fare freddo OR avere freddo *to be cold*

Some aspects of the weather have their own verbs:

piovere *to rain*   Piove. *It is raining.*
nevicare *to snow*   Nevica. *It is snowing.*

THE VERB "TO KNOW"

There are two verbs to express the idea "to know": **sapere** and **conoscere. Sapere** means "to know" in the sense of knowing a *fact* or knowing *how to do something.* **Conoscere** is used when the sense is "to know" a person or in general cases of familiarity.

Sanno quando veniamo (OR, verremo)? *Do they know when we are coming?*

Sai giocare a carte? *Do you know how to play cards?*

Conosco Maria molto bene. *I know Mary very well.*

Non conosco Roma. *I'm not familiar with Rome.*

PRONOUNS; MODAL AUXILIARIES; PREPOSITIONS BEFORE INFINITIVES; MORE IRREGULAR VERBS: VOLERE, POTERE, DOVERE?

THE OBJECT PRONOUNS

A pronoun substitutes for the noun. The *direct* object pronoun will answer the questions Who? and What? The *indirect* object pronoun will answer the questions To whom? and For whom? Instead of saying "We see the book," one can say "we see it." Notice that in Italian the characteristic position of the object projouns, direct and indirect, is before the verb, just as with the reflexive pronoun (explained in topic 9).

THE DIRECT OBJECT PRONOUNS in Italian and English are:

mi	*me*
ti	*you* (informal)
lo	*him, it* (masculine)
la	*her, it* (feminine)
La	*you* (formal)
ci	*us*
vi	*you* (informal)
li	*them* (masculine)
le	*them* (feminine)
Li	*you* (formal masculine)
Le	*you* (formal feminine)

For example:
1. Vediamo *il libro. Lo* vediamo.
   (We see *the book*. We see *it*.)
2. Comprano *le reviste. Le* comprano.
   (They buy *the magazines*. They buy *them*.)
3. Tengo *le chiavi. Le* tengo.
   (I keep *the keys*. I keep *them*.)
4. Do *gli esami. Li* do.
   (I am taking *the exams*. I am taking *them*.)

Notice this change in the forms of the direct object pronouns: **Mi, ti, lo, la, vi** omit their vowel before another vowel and the letter *h*. The apostrophe is substituted for the missing vowel.

1. Insegno *la lezione*. *L'*insegno.
   (I am teaching *the lesson*. I am teaching *it*.)
2. Hanno visto *lo spettacolo*. *L'*hanno visto.
   (They have seen *the show*. They have seen *it*.)

THE INDIRECT OBJECT PRONOUN. The indirect object pronouns in Italian and in English are:

mi	*to, for me*
ti	*to, for you* (informal)
gli	*to, for him; to, for it* (masculine); *to, for them*
le	*to, for her; to, for it* (feminine)
Le	*to, for you* (formal, masculine and feminine)
ci	*to, for us*
vi	*to, for you* (informal)
loro	*to, for them* (masculine and feminine)
Loro	*to, for you* (formal, masculine and feminine)

For example:

1. Mando il regalo *a Giovanni*. *Gli* mando il regalo.
   (I'm sending the gift *to John*. I'm sending the gift *to him*.)
2. Diamo tutto *a Marta*. *Le* diamo tutto.
   (We give everything *to Marta*. We give everything *to her*.)
3. Presta dei soldi *a me*. *Mi* presta dei soldi.
   (She is lending some money *to me*. She is lending *me* some money.)
4. Faccio una domanda *a loro*. Faccio *loro* una domanda. OR *Gli* faccio una domanda.
   (I am asking a question *of them*. I'm asking *them* a question.)
5. Comprano i fiori *a te*. *Ti* comprano i fiori.
   (They buy flowers *for you*. They buy *you* flowers.)

Notice this change in the forms of the indirect object pronouns: **Mi, ti, vi** omit their vowel before another vowel and the letter *h*, and the apostrophe is substituted for the missing vowel.

Mi invia i migliori saluti. (He sends *me* best wishes.)
*M'*invia i migliori saluti.

Position of Object Pronouns

1. the formula. The combination of a direct and an indirect object will always result in the following formula: IO + DO + V (Indirect Object plus Direct Object plus Verb). Some changes in the spelling of the combination may take place, as the following lists indicate:

me lo	me la	glieli	gliele	ve lo	ve la
me li	me le	se lo	se la	ve li	ve le
te lo	te la	se li	se le	se lo	se la
te li	te le	ce lo	ce la	se li	se le
glielo	gliela	ce li	ce le		

2. exceptions. The two indirect pronouns, **loro** and **Loro,** do not enter this list because of course they *follow* the verb with a direct object pronoun.

Lui vende loro la mạcchina. *He sells them the car.*

Lui la vende loro, *or* Gliela vende. *He sells it to them.*

3. spelling changes. Notice that in the preceding lists certain changes have occurred in the spelling of some forms:
(a) **Mi, ti, ci,** and **vi** change *i* to *e* before **lo, la, li,** and **le.**
(b) **Gli** becomes **glie** before **lo, la, li,** and **le,** which are added to it.

Gliele mando. *I send them to him.* (*Gli*—to him—has become *glie* before *le* which is joined to it.)

Mi legge la lẹttera. *He reads me the letter.*

Me la legge. *He reads it to me.* (*Mi* changes to *me* before *la*.)

The Disjunctive Pronoun

The main group of disjunctive pronouns comprises those which are utilized with a preposition in a prepositional phrase. These prepositional pronouns in Italian and in English are:

me	*me*
te	*you* (informal, singular)
lui	*him*
lei	*her*
Lei	*you* (formal, singular)
se	*himself, herself, itself, yourself*

noi	*us*
voi	*you* (informal, plural)
loro	*them*
Loro	*you* (formal, plural)
se	*themselves, yourselves*

1. USE OF "SE." **Se** is used only when this prepositional object is the same person as the subject.

Lo fa da sè. *He does it by himself.*

Conversa con noi. *He is chatting with us.*

In addition to the regular use of the prepositional pronouns, the forms may be substituted for clarity, contrast, or emphasis when two object pronouns are involved.

Vede me, non te. *He sees me, not you.*

2. USES OF "SI." Notice the importance of the grave accent in written Italian, as illustrated by the word **si**:

(a) *sì:* to mean "yes."

(b) *si* compra: one, you, people (as an indefinite person) buy.

(c) *si* vede: reflexive object used as a substitute for the passive when no agent is expressed (it is seen, one sees).

(d) *sì:* sometimes as *thus, so, as.*

THE DEMONSTRATIVE PRONOUN

The demonstrative pronouns, which take the place of a demonstrative adjective or a noun, have the same inflections as the demonstrative adjectives given in Topic 16.

	Singular	*Plural*
1. *"This (one)," "these"*		
masculine:	questo	questi
feminine:	questa	queste
2. *"That (one)," "those"*		
masculine:	quello	quelli
feminine:	quella	quelle

Preferisco questo libro, non quel libro.
I prefer this book, not that book.

Preferisco questo, non quello.
I prefer this one, not that one. (book)

THE POSSESSIVE PRONOUN

These have the same forms as the possessive adjectives, listed in Topic 6. The noun is, of course, omitted.

Usiamo il nostro passaporto e Carlo usa il suo passaporto. (adjective) *We are using our passport and Charles is using his passport.*

Usiamo il nostro e Carlo usa il suo. (pronoun) *We are using ours, and Charles is using his.*

ANALOGIES OF THE REFLEXIVE, INDIRECT, AND DIRECT OBJECT PRONOUNS

SIMILARITIES OF FORM

1. The reflexive, indirect, and direct object pronouns will have the *same* forms in the first and second persons singular and plural: **mi, ti, ci, vi.**
2. In the third person singular and plural, the reflexive object pronoun will have the same form: **si.**
3. Note that the forms **c'è** (there is) and **ci sono** (there are) reflect the use of **ci** meaning "there" rather than "us" or "to us."

CONJUNCTIVE PRONOUN/PARTITIVE

Ne takes the place of the prepositional phrase which begins with **di.** **Ne** is placed before the verb.

    1. Mangia *della carne. Ne* mangia. *(She is eating some meat. She is eating some of it.)*

    2. Compro *del latte. Ne* compro un po'. *(I buy some milk. I buy a little of it.)*

Observe that the partitive construction *must* be inserted in Italian though it is often hidden in English.

    Le matite? Quante ne vuoi? *The pencils? How many (of them) do you want?*

MODAL AUXILIARIES

These are verbs, such as **potere, volere,** and **dovere,** which stand alone before an infinitive and often require the infinitive to complete their thought.

    Non voglio parlare. *I don't want to speak.*

    Non può venire. *He can't come.*

Prepositions Before Infinitives

Many verbs do not require a preposition before an infinitive (including the *modals*).

Preferisco venire con te. *I prefer to come with you.*

However, some verbs call for the preposition **a** before a dependent infinitive. These verbs are usually: (a) verbs of beginning, preparing, or continuing; (b) verbs of motion; and (c) verbs of learning or instruction. Other categories should be learned as they appear.

Comincia a studiare la lezione.

He is beginning to study the lesson.

Vengo a trovare un mio amico.

I'm going to see a friend of mine.

Impariamo a scrivere molte lettere.

We are learning to write many letters.

Many verbs require the use of the preposition **di** before an infinitive. Their categories and usages are highly varied, but some general classifications are: (a) verbs of command and request; (b) verbs of trying; (c) verbs of hope and belief; and (d) some verb + noun formations.

Ti prega di non andare a casa. *He begs you not to go home.*

Cerchiamo di capire. *We are trying to understand.*

Credono di poter partire presto. *They believe they will be able to leave soon.*

Ho bisogno di venire con voi. *I need to come with you* (pl).

Note that **da** before an infinitive normally denotes purpose.

Cosa c'è da fare? *What is there to do?* (that needs to be done)

More Irregular Verbs

Three verbs introduced previously as *modal verbs* (**volere, potere,** and **dovere**) are irregular. Their *future stems* as well as their present indicative forms should be noted.

	Present	*Future*
volere	voglio	vorrò
	vuoi	etc.
	vuole	

	vogliamo	
	volete	
	vọgliono	
potere	posso	po*tr*ò
	puoi	etc.
	può	
	possiamo	
	potete	
	pọssono	
dovere	devo	do*vr*ò
	devi	etc.
	deve	
	dobbiamo	
	dovete	
	dẹvono	

THE PAST PARTICIPLE; PRESENT, FUTURE, AND CONDITIONAL PERFECT TENSES; PAST PARTICIPLE: ABSOLUTE CONSTRUCTION AND ADJECTIVES

The Italian verb is formed in three ways:

1. By using the stem of the infinitive after dropping the ending, as in the present, imperfect, and preterit tenses.

2. By using the complete infinitive to which a set of endings is added, as in the future and conditional tenses.

3. By using a helping verb (**avere** or **essere**) plus the past participle to form compound tenses.

From this third combination five additional tenses in the indicative may be created, three of which we will see in this Topic: the *passato prossimo* (the present perfect), the *futuro anteriore* (the future perfect), and the *condizionale passato* (the conditional perfect).

THE PAST PARTICIPLE

The past participle is formed regularly in the way indicated below, while for some verbs the past participle is formed irregularly.

REGULAR FORMATION

Verb	Stem	Ending	Past Participle
parlare	parl +	ato =	parlato *spoken*
vendere	vend +	uto =	venduto *sold*
capire	cap +	ito =	capito *understood*

To the stem of the infinitive (infinitive minus the ending) is added the new ending: *-ato* for the first conjugation; *-uto* for the second conjugation; and *-ito* for the third conjugation.

Note the equivalent part of speech in English (**parlato**—spoken). Remember that the past participle does *not* stand alone as a verb form (except in the Absolute construction seen at the end of this Topic). It must be accompanied by the helping verb.

IRREGULAR FORMATION: A partial list of irregular past participles with their infinitives follows.

Infinitive	*Past Participle*
aprire	aperto
morire	morto
bere	bevuto
offrire	offerto
chiędere	chiesto
pręndere	preso
chiụdere	chiuso
rimanere	rimasto
dire	detto
scrịvere	scritto
fare	fatto
vedere	visto (veduto)
lęggere	letto
venire	venuto
mettere	messo
vịvere	vissuto

THE PRESENT PERFECT TENSE
(Il passato prossimo)

The present perfect tense of **parlare** is:

ho parlato	*I have spoken*
hai parlato	*you have spoken*
ha parlato	*he, she (you) (has or have) spoken*
abbiamo parlato	*we have spoken*
avete parlato	*you have spoken*
hanno parlato	*they have spoken*

The present perfect tense of **vęndere** is:

ho venduto	*I have sold*
hai venduto	*you have sold*
ha venduto	*he, she (you) (has or have) sold*
abbiamo venduto	*we have sold*
avete venduto	*you have sold*
hanno venduto	*they have sold*

The present perfect tense of **capire** is:

ho capito	*I have understood*
hai capito	*you have understood*
ha capito	*he, she (you) (has or have) understood*
abbiamo capito	*we have understood*
avete capito	*you have understood*
hanno capito	*they have understood*

FORMATION WITH AUXILIARY VERBS. The majority of verbs use **avere** as an auxiliary verb in the present perfect tense; for example, all transitive verbs (those which take a direct object) use **avere.** But some verbs are not conjugated with **avere,** but with **essere.** For example, intransitive verbs (those which do *not* take a direct object) generally require **essere;** and most verbs of motion take **essere.** The following verbs are the most common ones which employ **essere** instead of **avere** as the helping verb in the compound tenses.

andare	*to go*
arrivare	*to arrive*
cadere	*to fall*
correre	*to run*
entrare	to enter
morire	*to die*
nascere	*to be born*
partire	*to leave*
restare	*to stay*
ritornare	*to return*
salire	*to go up*
scendere	to go down
stare	*to be*
uscire	*to go out*
venire	*to come*

Thus the present perfect tense of the verb **venire** will consist of the present tense of the verb **essere** and the past participle of the verb **venire.**

sono venuto/a	*I have come*
sei venuto/a	*you have come*
è venuto/a	*he, she (you) (have or has) come*
siamo venuti/e	*we have come*

	siete venuti/e	*you have come*
	sono venuti/e	*they have come*

AVERE AND ESSERE. The verbs ẹssere and avere as main verbs require the helping verb ẹssere and avere respectively. The present perfect tense of these two verbs in thus:

avere	ho avuto	*I have had*
	hai avuto	*you have had*
	ha avuto	*he, she (you) (has or have) had*
	abbiamo avuto	*we have had*
	avete avuto	*you have had*
	hanno avuto	*they have had*
ẹssere	sono stato/a	*I have been*
	sei stato/a	*you have been*
	è stato/a	*he, she (you) (has or have) been*
	siamo stati/e	*we have been*
	siete stati/e	*you have been*
	sono stati/e	*they have been*

Note: The endings of **stato,** just as those of **venuto,** are marked by *a, i,* and *e,* so that the respective past participles are: **stato, stata, stati, state; venuto, venuta, venuti, venute.**

RULES OF AGREEMENT.

1. A past participle conjugated with the verb ẹssere agrees in *gender* and *number* with the subject. The change in spelling to achieve agreement is the same as that for regular nouns *o, a, i, e.*

2. A past participle conjugated with the verb **avere** agrees with the direct object when it is a person and comes before the verb. Agreement is compulsory if the pronouns **lo, la, li, le** and **ne** precede the verb. If the direct object is not a person but still comes before the verb, agreement is optional.

Non abbiamo studiato l'italiano. *We have not studied Italian.* OR *We did not study Italian.*

Sono andati a casa sua. *They have gone to his house.*

L'ho veduta. *I have seen her.* OR *I saw her.*

PRESENT PERFECT AND PERTERIT. The present perfect tense, besides the literal translation as a compound verb, may be rendered as the preterit tense in English. In fact, conversational and general usage in Italian prefers the present perfect tense to the preterit tense. For example, the Italian phrase "Gli ho scritto ieri" is translated most idiomatically by using the English preterit: "I wrote to him yesterday" (instead of *I have written*). Yet in this case spoken Italian prefers the use of the present perfect and not the preterit.

THE FUTURE PERFECT AND CONDITIONAL PERFECT TENSES
(*Il futuro anteriore* e *Il condizionale passato*)

The *future perfect* tense is formed by using the future tense of **avere** or **essere** plus the past participle.

MODEL VERBS. The model verb **parlare** becomes:

avrò parlato	*I shall have spoken*
avrai parlato	*you will have spoken*
avrà parlato	*he, she (you) will have spoken*
avremo parlato	*we shall have spoken*
avrete parlato	*you will have spoken*
avranno parlato	*they will have spoken*

The future perfect tense of **venire** is:

sarò venuto/a	*I shall have come*
sarai venuto/a	*you will have come*
sarà venuto/a	*he, she (you) will have come*
saremo venuti/e	*we shall have come*
sarete venuti/e	*you will have come*
saranno venuti/e	*they will have come*

The *conditional perfect* tense is formed by using the conditional tense of **avere** or **essere** plus the past participle.

MODEL VERBS. The regular verb **parlare** of the first conjugation becomes:

avrei parlato	*I should have spoken*
avresti parlato	*you would have spoken*
avrebbe parlato	*he, she (you) would have spoken*
avremmo parlato	*we should have spoken*
avreste parlato	*you would have spoken*
avrebbero parlato	*they would have spoken*

The conditional perfect tense of **venire** is:

sarei venuto/a	*I should have come*
saresti venuto/a	*you would have come*

sarebbe venuto/a   *he, she (you) would have come*
saremmo venuti/e   *we should have come*
sareste venuti/e   *you would have come*
sarębbero venuti/e   *they would have come*

OTHER USES OF THE FUTURE AND CONDITIONAL PERFECT. In addition to the regular use of the future perfect and conditional perfect tenses to translate English equivalents of the same meaning, there are some additional uses in Italian of these tenses.

1. *Probability* or *possibility* in the present perfect tense is rendered by the future perfect tense in Italian.

Avremo perduto la busta. *We have probably lost the envelope.*

2. *Implication.* When the future perfect and the conditional perfect tenses are implied in English, they must be utilized in Italian.

Ha detto che sarębbero arrivati ormai. *He said that they would have arrived by now.*

PAST PARTICIPLE: ABSOLUTE CONSTRUCTION AND ADJECTIVES

The past participle may stand alone (without a helping verb) when it functions (1) in an *absolute* construction, and (2) as an *adjective*. For example:

1. *Scritte* due lęttere, ho cominciato a studiare l'italiano.
   (*Having written two letters,* I *began studying Italian.*)
2. *Arrivata* a casa, Marta è andata a letto.
   (*Having gotten home, Marta went to bed.*)
3. Impariamo la lingua *scritta* e la lingua *parlata*.
   (*We are learning the written language and the spoken language.*)

Note that in Example 1, **scritte** (from **scrivere**) must agree with its direct object, **lęttere** (feminine plural). All transitive verbs used in this construction follow this rule. In Example 2, **arrivata** (from **arrivare**—an intransitive verb) agrees with the subject who has already arrived home. Finally, in Example 3, we see **scritta** and **parlata** functioning as adjectives modifying **lingua.**

REVIEW EXERCISES, TOPICS 8–11

PATTERN DRILLS. Use the following infinitives in these tenses to complete the sentences. (a) present, (b) present perfect, (c) future, (d) future perfect, (e) conditional, and (f) conditional perfect.

1. Il professore non (venire) in classe.

2. Oggi tutti (divertirsi) molto.
3. Quando (potere) Lei leggere il mio giornale?
4. Noi (conoscere) a poco a poco la nuova studentessa francese.
5. Voi (volere) rimanere a casa?
6. Io (continuare) a tenere a mente la poesia latina.
7. Lo studente inglese (dovere) parlare tedesco.
8. Noi (prendere) il treno che (partire) alle otto e dieci.

TRANSLATE the following into Italian:

1. What time is it? It's 5:30 in the morning, more or less.
2. Where are the Italian books? We shall give them to him.
3. These houses painted blue and white are interesting—we ought to visit them.
4. Do you need to buy some milk? (*Lei*)
5. This flower seems large and beautiful, but the garden is very small.
6. Do you have your sweater? I have mine, and he has his.
7. There are many large buildings in Rome.
8. Where are you? I'm here.
9. Having had (*prendere*) a coffee, I went home.
10. Now there is only a little money.
11. Today is November 1, 1982.
12. I am going to leave on the second Sunday in January. But as always I'll be back on the next Wednesday.
13. I always want to get there at 3:45 sharp.
14. How old is John? He is probably twenty-four years old. However, according to him, he's only twenty.
15. She sold them to Mary. Did you buy them?
16. Can I give you a hand?
17. I have understood everything you're doing.
18. Have you already drunk yours?
19. He put (*mettere*) the money in his pocket.
20. They saw her twice yesterday.

TRANSLATE the following into Italian:

1. Did you understand that we have to go to their house?
2. She needs a pair of shoes.
3. He had a good time since (*siccome*) he knows how to play the piano.
4. They will have sold everything.
5. I'm sending it to him.

6. They see us often.
7. Do you know who they are? Yes, I know them.
8. Only Italian is spoken here.
9. I'm putting on my gloves.
10. We will not have understood the written word.

THE SUBJUNCTIVE: FORMATION OF PRESENT AND PRESENT PERFECT FORMS; IRREGULAR VERBS

The *subjunctive* (*congiuntivo*) indicates a *mood* (see Topic 4), and thus conveys the intention of the user of the verb. For the moment it is enough to remember that this mood expresses what is *not* a certainty. Within the subjunctive mood there are four basic tenses of interest to us, two of which will be explored in this Topic. The formation of the *present* and *present perfect* subjunctive should be learned as thoroughly as their parallel tenses in the indicative mood.

THE PRESENT SUBJUNCTIVE

The present subjunctive tense of four model verbs is:

parlare	parl*i*	parl*iamo*
	parl*i*	parl*iate*
	parl*i*	p*a*rl*ino*
v*e*ndere	vend*a*	vend*iamo*
	vend*a*	vend*iate*
	vend*a*	v*e*nd*ano*
servire	serv*a*	serv*iamo*
	serv*a*	serv*iate*
	serv*a*	s*e*rv*ano*
capire	capisc*a*	cap*iamo*
	capisc*a*	cap*iate*
	capisc*a*	cap*i*scano

A brief systematic arrangement of this tense will reveal interesting and helpful similarities and differences with regard to its parallel tense in the indicative. (See also p. 18, Topic 5.)

	-are	*-ere*	*-ire*	
			(a)	(b)
io	-i	-a	-a	-isc*a*

tu	-i	-a	-a	-isc*a*
lei/lui	-i	-a	-a	-isc*a*
noi	-iamo	-iamo	-iamo	-iamo
voi	-iate	-iate	-iate	-iate
loro	-*i*no	-*a*no	-*a*no	-isc*a*no

The most striking feature of the present subjunctive is the repetition of the first three endings for the singular persons. This possible point of confusion *often necessitates the use of the subject pronouns* (**io, tu, lei/lui**) for clarification. Note also the invariable forms of first and second plural (*iamo* and *iate* throughout), while the third person plural admits but *one* variation: *i*no, *a*no, *a*no, **isc*a*no**.

AVERE AND ESSERE. The present subjunctive forms of **avere** and **essere** are:

avere	abbia	abbiamo	**essere**	sia	siamo
	abbia	abbiate		sia	siate
	abbia	abbiano		sia	siano

TTHE PRESENT PERFECT SUBJUNCTIVE

The present perfect subjunctive (*passato prossimo congiuntivo*) is constructed on the same principle as its compound counterpart in the indivative. The auxiliary verb (**avere** or **essere**) conjugated in the present subjunctive is combined with the past participle of the principal verb.

MODEL VERBS. The present perfect subjunctive of three model verbs is:

parlare	abbia parlato	abbiamo parlato
	abbia parlato	abbiate parlato
	abbia parlato	abbiano parlato
vendere	abbia venduto	abbiamo venduto
	abbia venduto	abbiate venduto
	abbia venduto	abbiano venduto
servire	abbia servito	abbiamo servito
	abbia servito	abbiate servito
	abbia servito	abbiano servito

NOTE 1. In the present perfect, the verb **capire** does not differ from the model **servire:** that is, **ạbbia capito,** and so forth.

2. Again, for clarification the subject pronouns should be used for the first three persons of the verb.

3. The typical verb **arrivare,** conjugated with ẹssere, must have the past principle in agreement with the subject, as in the indicative mood. Thus the present perfect subjunctive of **arrivare** would be:

sia arrivato/a   siamo arrivati/e
sia arrivato/a   siate arrivati/e
sia arrivato/a   sịano arrivati/e

IRREGULAR VERBS

One essential point should be remembered regarding the formation of irregular verbs in the present subjunctive. Normally, the verb may be arrived at by taking the verb's *first person singular* (io) *form* of the present indicative and substituting the present subjunctive ending.

t3

	Indicative	*Subjunctive*	
venire	vengo	venga	veniamo
		venga	veniate
		venga	vẹngạno
dire	dico	dica	diciamo
		dica	diciate
		dica	dịcạno

But note the irregular nature of **andare** and **dare.**

t3

	Indicative	*Subjunctive*	
andare	*vado*	vada	andiamo
		vada	andiate
		vada	vạdano
dare	ḍo	dịa	diamo
		dia	diate
		dia	dịano

In the meantime all these verbs are formed "regularly" in the present perfect subjunctive, employing the proper helping verb.

Sia venuto/a   ạbbia detto

sia andato/a   ạbbia dato

USES OF THE SUBJUNCTIVE

Recalling Topic 12, we must remember that the subjunctive mood expresses the uncertain, the hypothetical. Its use in a sentence is usually dependent upon the presence of another grammatical element which conditions and demands the use of the subjunctive mood. Verbs in a main clause which express, in general, emotion, desire, doubt, or opinion, as well as impersonal expressions, will require the use of the subjunctive in the subordinate clause—usually introduced by **che** (that, who, which).

REQUIRED USAGES

The basic categories in which the use of the subjunctive mood is obligatory should be studied carefully. The subjunctive is *required* following verbs of:

1. EMOTION including hope, fear, happiness, sorrow, and so forth.

Maria ha paura *che* Lei non *venga* domani sera. *Maria is afraid that you'll not come tomorrow evening.*

Spero *che siate* contenti. *I hope that you are happy.*

Mi dispiace *che* non mi *abbia scritto* lui. *I'm sorry that he hasn't written me.*

2. VOLITION (wishing or wanting).

Vogliamo *che* tutti si *divertano. We want everybody to have a good time.*

Voglio *che* lei *venga* verso le otto. *I want her to come around eight.*

3. DOUBT, BELIEF, OPINION.

Dubito *che* me *abbiano mandato* il pacco chiesto. *I doubt that they sent me the package I asked for.*

Credo *che* voi *abbiate avuto* ragione. *I think/believe that you were right.*

Penso *che* lui *debba* andarci al più presto possibile. *I think he ought (dovere) to go there as soon as possible.*

But note the following exceptions:

If one is certain of facts, then the future or the present *indicative* (depending upon the initial verb) may be substituted for the present subjunctive.

Credo *che* lui *verrà* a frequentare le lezioni. *I think he'll come to attend class.*

Non dubito *che* arrivano in anticipo. *I don't doubt that they are arriving early.*

Note also that if the subject does *not* change, the subjunctive is replaced by an infinitive.

Penso di andare in montagna. *I think that I will go to the mountains.*

Not:

Penso che vada in montagna.

4. IMPERSONAL EXPRESSIONS.

È *meglio che* io *telefoni* a lei prima di partire. *It's better that I telephone her before leaving.*

È *possibile che* Claudia non *sia partita* ieri sera? *Is it possible that Claudia might not have left last night?*

Note: When the subject is impersonal (it) in both clauses, the subjunctive is *not* required but is substituted for by the *infinitive*.

È possibile *fare* una conferenza subito. *It is possible to give a lecture immediately.*

OTHER USES

Other uses and grammatical conditions which involve the subjunctive are:

1. SUPERLATIVES (see Topic 16).

Questa è la più bella casa che io *abbia* mai *vista*. *This is the most beautiful house I've ever seen.*

2. INDEFINITE EXPRESSIONS following *whatever* and *whoever*.

checchè	*whatever*	il primo che	*the first who*
chiunque	*whoever*	il solo che	*the only one who*
		l'ultimo che	*the last one who*

Checchè *facciano,* non riuscirà. *Whatever they do, it won't work out.*

3. BENCHÈ AND SEBBENE (although, even though).

Benchè io sia partito presto, sono arrivato in ritardo. *Even though I left early, I arrived late.*

4. INDEFINITE ANTECEDENTS.

Cerco una segretaria *che sappia* l'italiano. *I'm looking for a secretary who knows Italian.*

But notice the change in *mood* conditioned by a definite antecedent:

Conosco una signorina che sa molto bene l'italiano. *I know a young woman who knows Italian very well.*

5. VERBS OF COMMANDING, FORBIDDING, AND REQUEST.

Vi dico che *finiate* l'esame sụbito. *I'm telling you to finish the exam immediately.*

But with *no* command implied:

Vi dico che questo esame è molto diffịcile. *I'm telling you that this exam is very difficult.*

RELATIVE PRONOUNS; FURTHER USES OF PREPOSITIONS; IMPERSONAL VERBS

USES OF RELATIVE PRONOUNS

The relative pronoun is of special use in extending sentence construction beyond the simple SUBJECT-VERB-OBJECT pattern. With these relative pronouns, complex sentences can be constructed with ease. But keep in mind the difference between Italian *and* English usage: In Italian the relative pronoun must be used *at all times.*

THE FORMS of the relative pronoun are:
1. **che** (that, who, whom, which) never changes and may be used as the subject or the direct object.

Conosco Pietro *che* legge bene il francese. *I know Peter, who reads French well.*

2. **cui** (whom, which, whose).

(a) Used with a preposition:

Ecco il ristorante *in cui* mangiamo bene. *Here is the restaurant in which (where) we eat well.*

(b) **Cui** may also be used as a relative adjective when accompanied by the definite article and a noun (whose).

È Giovanni *il cui* padre torna in Italia. *It is Giovanni whose father is returning to Italy.*

3. In case of ambiguity **cui** and **che** may be substituted for: **il quale, la quale, i quali, le quali.**

La nipote di mio marito *la quale* sta seduta in classe ha undici anni. (*La quale* refers to the *niece.*) *My husband's niece who is seated in class is eleven years old.*

4. **Quello che, quel che, ciò che** (what).

Sappiamo *ciò che* pensa lui. *We know what he thinks.*

5. **Chi** may be used for the indefinite person (he who, the one who, etc.).

Chi dorme non piglia pesci. *He who sleeps doesn't catch fish. (The early bird catches the worm.)*

PREPOSITIONS

ESSENTIAL PROPOSITIONS which are used continually are:

a	*at, in, to*	in	*in, to, within*
con	*with*	lungo	*along*
da	*from, by*	per	*by, through*
di	*of*	su	*on, upon*
durante	*during*	tra *or* fra	*among, between*

PREPOSITIONS WITH "A." Propositions which are generally followed by the additional preposition **a** are:

accanto a	*beside*	in faccia a	*opposite*
attorno a	*around*	in mezzo a	*amidst*
circa (a) or		in rispetto a *or*	
incirca (a)	*about*	inquanto a	*concerning*
conforme a	*in conformity with*	innanzi a *or*	
		dinanzi a *or*	
dentro a	*inside*	davanti a	*before*
dietro a *or*		intorno a	*about*
di dietro a	*behind*	vicino a	*near*
fino a	*as far as, until*		

PREPOSITIONS WITH "DA." Prepositions which are generally followed by the additional preposition **da** are:

fin da	*from*
lontano da	*far from*

1. **Da** is sometimes put before an infinitive. The preposition **da** serves to indicate purpose or necessity, meaning literally *for* . . . but rendered idiomatically always as *to* + verb.

Hanno molto *da* fare. *They have a lot to do.**

*Note that this construction usually follows a noun. If not, a noun is understood.

Ho *da* fare. *I have things I have to do.*

2. **Da** also functions idiomatically to mean *at the home of, at the shop of,* etc.

Vai *da* Francesco? *Are you going to Francesco's house?*

PREPOSITIONS WITH "DI." Prepositions which are generally followed by the additional preposition **di** are:

a causa di	by reason of, because
a dispetto di	in spite of
a forza di	by dint of
a piè di	at the foot of
a ragione di	on account of
a modo di	in the manner of
a secondo di	according to
al di là di	on the other side of, beyond
al di qua di	on this side of
al di sopra di	above
alla volta di	in the direction of
all'infuori di	except
di dentro	within
di fuori	outside
di sotto	underneath
fuori di	outside of
in favore di	in favor of
in luogo di, *or* invece *di*	instead of
per mezzo di	by means of
presso di	near
prima di	before

IMPERSONAL VERBS

Those verbs which express a state without reference to a person are called *impersonal verbs*. Usually these verbs are found only in the third person singular (it) and plural (they).

accadere (*to happen*): accade (*it happens*).

avvenire (*to happen*): è avvenuto (*it happened*).

bastare (*to be enough*): basta (*it is enough*), bastano (*they are sufficient*). Note: Ce ne bastano tre. (*Three of them are enough.*)

bisognare (*to be necessary*): bisogna (*it is necessary*). Note: Bisogna andarci subito. (*It is necessary to go there at once.*)

capitare (*to happen*): capita (*it happens*).

convenire (*to be fitting*): conviene (*it is fitting*). Note: Ti conviene. (*It fits you.*)

dovere essere (*to be obligatory*): dev'essere (*it must be*), dovrebb'essere (*it ought to be*). Note: Dev'essere vero. (*It must be true.*)

importare (*to matter*): importa (*it matters*); non importa (*it doesn't matter, or never mind*).

occorrere (*to be needed*): occorre (*it is needed*).

parere (*to appear, seem*): pare (*it appears, seems*). Note: Non ti pare vero? (*Doesn't it seem true to you?*)

*****piacere** (*to be pleasing*): piace (*it pleases*); piacciono (*they are pleasing*).

sembrare (*to seem*): sembra (*it seems*).

Note also:

addirsi (*to suit*): si addice (*it is suiting*).

essere lecito (*to be allowed*): è lecito (*it is allowed*).

*****Piacere** means literally "to be pleasing." Thus to render the English "I like it," the phrase must be recognized in its Italian construction:

Mi *piace* il nuovo film.

(Literally: *To me the new film is pleasing.*)

(Idiomatic: *I like the new film.*)

Note the change in the verb to the plural for objects which "are liked."

Mi *piacciono* i fiori. (*Fiori* is the subject of *piacere*.) (*I like the flowers.*)

IMPERSONAL VERBS IN WEATHER EXPRESSIONS. Impersonal verbs are also used in weather expressions: see Topic 9.

fioccare (*to fall in flakes*): fiocca (*Flakes are falling.*)

gelare (*to freeze*): gela (*It is freezing.*)

lampeggiare (*to lightning*): lampeggia (*There is lightning.*)

nevicare (*to snow*): nevica (*It is snowing.*)

piovere (*to rain*): piove (*It is raining.*)

sgelare (*to thaw*): sgela (*It is thawing.*)

tirare vento (*to be windy*): tira vento (*It is windy.*)

THE IMPERATIVE MOOD; POSITION OF OBJECT PRONOUNS; PARTICIPLES; USES OF THE PARTITIVE

THE IMPERATIVE MOOD

The third and final mood we will look at is the *imperative mood*. The imperative mood expresses a command which may be either affirmative or negative. (An exclamation point is often the indication of a command.) In this mood there is one tense: the present. Review the present indicative and subjunctive moods to help standardize the forms for any imperative construction.

The command forms corresponding to the subject pronouns **tu, Lei, noi, voi, Loro** (which are *not* inserted with the verb) are as follows for the model verbs of the three conjugations:

For the *-are* endings, using **parlare:**

	Indicative	*Imperative*	*Subjunctive*
io	parlo	—	parli
tu	parli	parla	parl*i*
Lei	parla	parli	parli
noi	parliamo	parliamo	parliamo
voi	parlate	parlate	parliate
Loro	parlano	parlino	parlino

The *-ere* and *-ire* endings are alike. Note **capire.**

	Indicative	*Imperative*	*Subjunctive*
vendere	vendo	—	venda
	vendi	vendi	venda
	vende	venda	vend*a*
	vendiamo	vendiamo	vendiamo
	vendete	vendete	vendiate
	vendono	vendano	vendano

	Indicative	Imperative	Subjunctive
servire	servo	—	serva
	servi	servi	serva
	serve	serva	serva
	serviamo	serviamo	serviamo
	servite	servite	serviate
	sęrvono	sęrvano	sęrvano

	Indicative	Imperative	Subjunctive
capire	capisco	—	capisca
	capisci	capisci	capisca
	capisce	capisca	capisca
	capiamo	capiamo	capiamo
	capite	capite	capiate
	capiscono	capiscano	capiscano

Clearly, the imperative mood may be formed with already existing forms of the indicative and subjunctive moods.

Ripetete ad alta voce. *Repeat—all of you—aloud.*

Mi *scriva* al più presto possịbile. *Please write me, Sir, as soon as possible.*

Ser*viamo* il caffè sụbito. *Let's serve the coffee immediately.*

Non partecipare a quello scherzo. *Don't take part in that joke.*

Note that **ęssere, sapere,** and **avere** use **siate, sappiate,** and **abbiate** (from the subjunctive instead of indicative) for the *voi* form command.

The complete imperative form of **avere** is:

> abbi (tu)
> ạbbia (lei)
> abbiamo
> abbiate
> ạbbiano (loro)

Abbi pazienza! *Be patient!*

POSITION OF OBJECT PRONOUNS

Note the following rules regarding placement of the object pronouns. (See also Topic 10.)

1. IN NEGATIVE SENTENCES, **non** precedes all object pronouns.

2. IN COMPOUND SENTENCES, the pronouns precede the auxiliary verbs.

3. PRECEDENCE. The object pronouns—direct, indirect, and reflexive—are placed *before* the verb except in the following cases where the pronouns *follow* and are *joined to* the verbs.

(a) The infinitive.

Lo vede Lei? *Do you see him?*

Vorremmo vederlo. *We would like to see him.*

Note: **Loro** and **loro** are, of course, exceptions.

Non potremo parlare loro domani. *We shall not be able to speak to them tomorrow.*

(b) The present participle.

scrivęndogli

(c) The past participle without auxiliary verb.

vedųtala

(d) The affirmative imperative (but not in the subjunctive).

Mạndamelo. *Send it to me.*

But in the polite command:

Me lo mandi. *Please send it to me.*

Note the relative positions of the direct and indirect object pronouns (see #4).

(e) with **ecco.**

Ęcco*lo. Here it is.*

(f) It is important to note that the original stress of the word to which pronouns are attached does not change. Thus:

scrivęndogli   vedųtala   mạndamelo

4. INDIRECT VS. DIRECT. When two pronouns come together (except **loro**) the *indirect* precedes the *direct*.

5. ELISIONS AND CHANGES

(a) **Me, ti, si, lo,** and **la** usually elide before verbs beginning with a vowel.

(b) **Mi, ti, si, ci,** and **vi** change i to e before **lo, la, li, le, ne.**

Me le dà.

Ce le racconta.

(c) **Gli** and **le,** before **lo, la, li, le, ne** become **glie,** which is joined to the object pronoun.

Glielo manderà.

Gliene compro.

(d) Before familiar commands (but not in the subjunctive) that have only one syllable, the initial consonant of the pronoun is doubled *except* for **gli.**

Dammi il cappello.

At this point, it would be wise to review Topic 10 on the object pronouns; the position of these pronouns with verbs; and the results when two objects come together in the same sentence.

PARTICIPLES

We have already seen the formation of one participle: the past participle (see Topic 11). Three remaining forms of participles will be taken up here.

1. GERUND. The first is the *gerundio* (gerund) which is often equivalent to the present participle in English. It is formed by dropping the infinitive ending and adding *-ando* (for *-are* verbs) or *-endo* (for *-ere* and *-ire* verbs).

The *gerundio* is used in its literal meaning.

Prend*endo* il treno, siamo partiti da Milano. *Taking the train, we left from Milan.*

It may also contain the idea of "on," "upon," "in," "by," and so forth.

Visitando la chiesa, ci siamo resi conto della ricchezza dell'architettura d'Italia. *By visiting the church we realized the richness of Italian architecture.*

2. OTHER GERUND FORM. A second form of the gerund may be used as a subject or object. It amounts to the placing of a definite article before an infinitive—always considered masculine. However, this form should be used sparingly at first.

Lo studiare è sempre difficile. *Studying is always difficult.*

3. VERBAL ADJECTIVE. Finally, the actual present participle carries little of the weight of the gerund in Italian, and is used as a verbal adjective. The form is constructed by dropping the infinitive ending and adding *-ante* (for *-are* verbs) or *-ente* (for *-ere* and *-ire* verbs). This is shown, using seguire—*seguente.*

Gli esempi *seguenti* sono facili. *The following examples are easy.*

Note: Particular attention should be given to the use and translation of the gerund.

1. *Aprendo* la finestra, ho visto la sua macchina grigia. (*Opening the window, I saw his gray car.*)

2. *Lavorando* per lo stato guadagno pochi soldi. (*By working for the state I earn little money.*)

3. Usciamo da casa mia, *urlando* come bestie. (*We leave my house, yelling like animals.*)

4. Direi che "pomodoro" vuol dire, *pensando* al vero senso della parola, "pomo d'oro." (*I would say that "pomodoro"—tomato— means, thinking about the true meaning of the word, "golden apple."*)

USES OF THE PARTITIVE

Two important means of expressing "some" or "a few" are: **qualche** and **alcuni (e)**. Note that **qualche** is always followed by a *singular* noun although it indicates "more than one," while **alcuni (e)** must be accompanied by a plural noun. There is no difference in their meanings.

qualche giorn*o a few days*
alcuni giorn*i a few days*

Thus, an expression such as "some" or "a few flowers" may be expressed: qualche fiore

alcuni fiori OR dei fiori
un po' di fiori

COMPARISONS: ADJECTIVES AND ADVERBS; CONJUNCTIONS

COMPARATIVES AND SUPERLATIVES

Both the adjective and the adverb have three degrees of comparison: positive, comparative, and superlative.

ENGLISH VS. ITALIAN.

In English, comparison is attained usually by the addition of the suffixes *er* or *est* to the adjective, as in "big, bigger, biggest." However, degree is also expressed by "more" and "most"; and by "less" and "least" for the diminishing quality.

In Italian, the comparisons are achieved by the addition of **più** and **il più** to the adjective for the expanding quality; and by the addition of **meno** and **il meno** for the diminishing quality.

REGULAR ADJECTIVES. A regular adjective is seen as:

	Positive	Comparative	Superlative
alto *tall*	alto	puì alto	il più alto
povero *poor*	povero	meno povero	il meno povero

IRREGULAR ADJECTIVES. The following adjectives of high frequency are irregular in comparison.

	Positive	Comparative	Superlative
alto *high*	alto	superiore	il superiore
basso *low*	basso	inferiore	l'inferiore
buono *good*	buono	migliore	il migliore
cattivo *bad*	cattivo	peggiore	il peggiore
esterno *external*	esterno	esteriore	l'esteriore
grande *big*	grande	maggiore	il maggiore
interno *internal*	interno	interiore	l'interiore
piccolo *little*	piccolo	minore	il minore

For example:

Il mędico è il più ricco figlio di tutta la famiglia. *The doctor is the richest son in the whole family.*

Questa minestra è migliore. *This soup is better.*

Note: The word "in" after the superlative degree is translated in Italian to the word **di** for "of."

THE ABSOLUTE SUPERLATIVE. There is also a degree of comparison beyond the superlative which is called the *absolute superlative*. It may be translated into English as "exceedingly," "extremely," "very," or "very, very."

Formation. The suffix -*issimo* is added to the adjective after the last vowel is eliminated.

> alto—altįssimo   bello—bellįssimo
> povero—poverįssimo   buono—buonįssimo

Some irregularities, however, characterize the formation of this absolute superlative:

(a) An adjective ending in -*co* or -*go* must insert the letter *h* to keep the original sound: bianco—bianchįssimo

(b) A few other adjectives have the ending -*ęrrimo.*

> acre (*sour*)—acęrrimo
> aspro (*harsh*)—aspęrrimo
> cęlebre (*famous*)—celebęrrimo
> įntegro (*honest*)—integęrrimo
> mįsero (*wretched*)—misęrrimo
> salubre (*healthy*)—salubęrrimo

(c) The following adverbs before an adjective will also give the expression the force of an absolute superlative.

> assai *rather*
> estremamente *extremely*
> immensamente *immensely*
> molto *very, very much*

(d) Note that often after the superlative one must use the subjunctive mood.

Questo è *il libro più interessante* che io *abbia* mai *letto. This is the most interesting book that I've ever read.*

ADVERBS

The adverb in Italian is usually formed by adding -*mente* to the feminine singular of the adjective. If the final syllable is *le* or *re,* then the *e* is omitted before adding -*mente*. And if the masculine and feminine forms in the singular are the same, then the suffix -*mente* is immediately placed on the form. This suffix in Italian corresponds to the English suffix "-ily."

rạpido (*rapid*)—rapidamente
fạcile (*easy*)—facilmente
felice (*happy*)—felicemente

ORDER OF THE ADVERB. The normal or grammatical order of the adverb is *after* the verb it modifies. The negative adverb **non** is of course an exception.

Scrive rapidamente. *He writes rapidly.*

COMPARISONS OF ADVERBS parallel those for adjectives: the quali-fying **più** or **meno** is used for the comparative, and the **il più** and **il meno** for the superlative.

rạpido, rapidamente
più rapidamente, il più rapidamente

ADVERBS IDENTICAL WITH ADJECTIVES. There are also some adjec-tives which achieve adverbial status without any change:

alto	*high*	forte	*strong*
basso	*low*	lungo	*long*
certo	*certain*	mezzo	*half*
chiaro	*clear*	piano	*soft*
corto	*short*	presto	*quick*
falso	*false*	sicuro	*sure*
fisso	*fixed*	spesso	*often*

ADVERBS WITH IRREGULAR COMPARISONS

	Positive	*Comparative*	*Superlative*
bene *well*	bene	meglio	il meglio
male *badly*	male	peggio	il peggio
molto *much*	molto	più	il più
poco *little*	poco	meno	il meno

ABSOLUTE ADVERBIAL SUPERLATIVE

1. *Regular.* The absolute superlative of the adverb is formed by adding -*mente* to the absolute superlative of the adjective which

ends in -*issimo*. However the feminine form, -*issima*, is then selected.

rapidissimo   rapidissimamente

2. *Irregular*. The four adverbs which have irregular comparisons also have irregular superlatives.

> bene—ottimamente
> male—pessimamente
> molto—moltissimo
> poco—pochissimo

COMPARISONS OF EQUALITY AND INEQUALITY

1. *Inequality*. **Di** or **che** is used with **di quel che** to express "than" before conjugated verbs.

(a) **Di** is used before modified nouns, pronouns, and numbers.

(b) **Che** is used before adjectives and adverbs.

(c) **Di quel che** is used only before conjugated verbs.

Questo museo è più ricco di quel museo. *This museum is richer than that museum.*

È più intelligente che generoso. *He is more intelligent than generous.*

La pellicola è più corta di quel che pensavo. *The roll of film is shorter than I thought.*

2. *Equality*. The expression of equal status is stated in one of two ways: (**così**) . . . **come** or (**tanto**) . . . **quanto**. (**Così** and **tanto** are often omitted in the formulas.) Note the variations and cases of agreement.

Hanno *tanto* denaro *quanto* il medico. *They have as much money as the doctor.*

Giovanni è alto *come* me. (*Così* has been omitted here.) *John is as tall as I.*

BUT Giovanna è alta *come* Gina. *Joan is as tall as Gina.*

Elena ha comprato *tante* matite *quante* penne. *Elaine bought as many pencils as she did pens.*

THE CONJUNCTION

The function of a conjunction is to *join* either (1) two words or clauses (coordinating conjunction), or (2) two clauses which are dependent upon one another (subordinating conjunction). The conjunction, which may be a single word or a compound form, clearly serves to link two ideas, and it will be most useful in the expression of more complex ideas and in the use of compound grammatical constructions.

In the following list, principal conjunctions are divided into two categories: simple and compound. Those conjunctions which require the use of the subjunctive are noted with an asterisk.

PRINCIPAL CONJUNCTIONS

1. *Simple:*

anche	*also, even, too*	mentre	*while*
ancora	*still, yet, again*	nè	*neither, nor*
anzi	*even, rather*	o	*or*
che	*that*	ossia	*or else*
cioè	*that is, that is to say*	però	*however*
come	*like, as*	pure	*really, still*
così	*thus, so*	quando	*when*
dunque	*then, so*	quasi*	*almost, as if*
e (ed)	*and*	quindi	*thus, so, therefore*
ma	*but*	se	*if*

Here are some presented in sentences:

Mi interessa tanto *anche* in rispetto a quell'aspetto storico. (*It interests me a lot even in relation to that historical aspect.*)

Sì, mi andrebbe una breve sosta, *cioè*, ho voglia di riposarmi. (*Yes, I could do with a short rest; in other words, I feel like resting.*)

Non sai *come* siamo contenti. (*You don't know how happy we are.*)

Mi ha chiesto di venire, e *dunque* ci sono andato. (*She asked me to come, and thus I went there.*)

2. *Compound:*

acciocchè*	*in order that*	neppure	*not even*
affinchè*	*in order that*	nonchè	*as well as*
allorchè*	*at the time when*	nonostante*	*notwithstanding*
allo stesso modo che	*in the same way that*	oppure	*or else*
		perchè	*because*
altresì	*likewise*	perciò	*therefore*
ancorchè*	*even if*	pertanto	*in fact*

benchè*	although	piuttosto che	rather than
caso mai che	if ever that	poichè	since
così . . . che	thus, so that	purchè*	provided
d'altra parte	on the other hand	qualora*	if
di modo che	so that	qualunque	whatever
e . . . e	both . . . and	quantunque*	although
finchè	until, as long as	sebbene*	although
fino a tanto che	as long as	senonchè	but
fuorchè	except	senza che*	without
giacchè	since	sia . . . sia	either . . . or
infatti	in fact	sicchè	since
inoltre	besides	siccome	inasmuch as
malgrado che*	despite that	supposto chè*	supposing that
nè . . . nè	neither . . . nor	tanto . . . che	so much . . . as
neanche	not even	tranne che	except that
nel caso che*	in case	tuttavia	yet, nevertheless

REVIEW EXERCISES, TOPICS 12–16

REVIEW PATTERN DRILLS. Use the following infinitives to complete the sentences in these tenses: present indicative, present perfect, future perfect, and conditional perfect.

1. I ragazzi non (alzarsi) puntualmente.
2. Noi (dovere) lęggere la lista attentamente.
3. Chi (volere) aiutarmi?
4. Lei non (riuscire) a spiegare l'esempio.
5. Io non lo (seguire).

Supply the proper indicative and subjunctive responses.

6. Io (credere) che lui non (venire).
7. Noi (pensare) che (essere) una buona idea.
8. Loro non (sapere) se voi (capire—present perfect).
9. Questa (essere) la più breve conferenza che io (vedere) mai.
10. Tu (volere) che io te ne (comprare) una copia?
11. Io (dubitare) che voi (avere) ragione.
12. Benchè non lo (capire—tu) (provare—imperative) a ascoltarlo.

TRANSLATE the following sentences into Italian:

1. He does not like to read the newspaper.
2. Give us the notebook!

3. Don't give it to them!
4. They have not realized the girl's identity.
5. She would like to return to Italy.
6. You have probably come too late.
7. New York is the richest city in the world.
8. But Rome is an extremely beautiful city also.
9. Dino is a better student than Mario, isn't he?
10. Entering his office, I saw the smallest and most beautiful painting in the world.
11. By reading a great deal, one learns to think clearly.
12. They have not returned it to them.
13. Is she not going to write me?
14. Are you willing to remain here?
15. Here are the beauties of the capital of Italy!
16. John and Mary have sat down quickly.
17. I've already read the book we talked about.
18. They probably would be in a hurry.
19. It's necessary to close the windows when it rains.
20. I excused myself and left the room.
21. They gave me as many problems as they did answers.
22. Please pass me the salt and pepper, Sir.
23. Don't listen to him! (*tu*)
24. Sit down and be patient! (*voi*)
25. She's smarter than he.
26. I believe I can do it.

SUPPLY THE CORRECT RESPONSE:

1. Io temo che (*he didn't understand you*) _____ (*very well*) _____ .
2. Penso che tu (*must pay him*) _____ (*what he wants*) _____ .
3. Chiunque (*telephones*) _____ (*say*) _____ di non venire oggi.
4. (*He who*) _____ insegna impara (*twice*) _____ .
5. Sebbene (*they have heard what*) _____ ho detto, continuano a sbagliare.
6. Lo stato (*of which*) _____ parlo è (*very far from your country*) _____ .
7. (*It is necessary*—bisognare) _____ che tu (*remember*) _____ la persona (*with whom*) _____ hai parlato.

8. Sua moglie (*whose letter*) _____ abbiamo letto, abita (*near us*) _____ .

9. (*In spite of the hand he gives me*) _____ ho troppo (*to do*) _____ .

10. (*Before leaving*) _____ (*it is enough*) _____ aprire una finestra.

11. (*Writing it to him*) _____ (*I am happier about it*) _____ .

12. La pagina (*following*) _____ ci va (*the best*) _____ .

13. (*Give me*) _____ il cappello, per favore.

14. (*Help me*) _____ e (*give it to me*) _____ :

15. (*Telephoning her*) _____ (*a few*) _____ giorno fa, mi sono reso conto del mio errore.

16. (*Please call me*) _____ .

17. (*Call them*) _____ :

18. (*Because she is the best student*) _____ , _____ ho dati (*them to her*).

19. (*Born in*) _____ Parigi, lei è (*as*) _____ contenta (*as*) _____ Giovanni.

20. Sembrano (*to be older*) _____ (*than*) _____ tu pensi.

21. Hai imparato (*the best*) _____ .

22. Giorgio ha (*a few good*) _____ idee, ma è (*less*) _____ intelligente (*than*) _____ coraggioso.

23. Vuole marinare la lezione senza che il professore (*noticing it*) _____ .

24. (*To you*) _____ lo spiega finchè (*you understand*) _____ .

25. Te l'ha spiegato finchè (*you understood*) _____ .

26. Malgrado che (*it is raining*) _____ , (*I still want*) _____ giocare a tennis.

PAST TIME: THE IMPERFECT AND THE PLUPERFECT

THE IMPERFECT

The formation of the *imperfect* in the indicative mood is regular for all verbs. It is accomplished by simply dropping the infinitive ending and adding the imperfect ending. Note the stress in third person plural.

parlare	parl	-*a*vo	parl-avamo
		avi	avate
		ava	parl-ạvano
vẹndere	vend	-*e*vo	vend-evamo
		evi	evate
		eva	vend-ẹvano
capire	cap	-*i*vo	cap-ivamo
		ivi	ivate
		iva	cap-ịvano

Note that each conjugation has the same set of endings except for the initial vowel of the ending. But this vowel, which changes, always reflects the "sign vowel" of the conjugation: *a* (-*are*), *e* (-*ere*) and *i* (-*ire*).

Notice that **avere** is conjugated regularly:

av*evo*	avevamo
avevi	avevate
aveva	avẹvano

But **ẹssere** represents one of the few irregular verbs in the tense:

ero	eravamo
eri	eravate
era	ẹrano

Finally, it should be noted that certain verbs require an irregular stem in the formation of the imperfect. For example, **fare**:

fac*evo*	facevamo
facevi	facevate
faceva	facęvano

THE IMPERFECT SUBJUNCTIVE is formed by adding the following endings to the same imperfect stem as found in the indicative:

parlare	parl-assi (io)	parl-assimo
	parl-assi (tu)	parl-aste
	parl-asse	parl-assero
vęndere	vend-essi	vend-ęssimo
	vend-essi	vendeste
	vend-esse	vend-ęssero
capire	cap-issi	cap-issimo
	cap-issi	cap-iste
	cap-isse	cap-issero

Again, **avere** is conjugated regularly, while **ęssere** is irregular.

avere	avessi	avęssimo	**ęssere**	fossi	fǫssimo
	avessi	aveste		fossi	foste
	avesse	avęssero		fosse	fǫssero

And notice how the imperfect subjunctive maintains the irregular stem of the indicative.

fare	*fa*cęssi	facęssimo
	facessi	faceste
	facesse	facęssero

The imperfect is one of the more difficult tenses for the English speaker, not with respect to its conjugation, but with regard to its usage. The simple imperfect has three possible renderings in English:

parlavo—*I spoke*
I was speaking
I used to speak

These three possibilities exist because the Italian tense is used to convey basically a *continuous action in the past*. Distinctions in this basic idea may include: description in the past, unfinished actions in the past, and even habitual states in the past. For example:

Pioveva al dirotto. (description) (*It was raining "cats and dogs."*)

Mentre Giovanni *cantava* una bella canzone francese, leggevo. (unfinished action) (*While John sang a beautiful French song, I read.*)

Fumavo tre anni fa, ma non fumo più. (habitual) (*I used to smoke three years ago, but I don't smoke anymore.*)

The force of certain verbs may vary from present perfect to imperfect, with the latter tense the preferred mode for expressing the more common features of that verb.

volere *to want*

Volevo due uova e burro da un etto. (*I was wanting two eggs and an etto* of butter.*)

Volevo expresses a general wanting, rendered in tone by the "I was wanting." Whereas an intense momentary desire would be expressed as: **Ho voluto** ("at that very moment") **due uova da lanciare.** ("I wanted two eggs I could throw.")

Other verbs which reflect this expressively tonal difference between the imperfect and the present perfect are: **dovere, pensare, desiderare,** and **credere.**

The imperfect subjunctive has much the same function as its indicative counterpart, but its use is somewhat wider and more dependent upon the sequence of tenses, as we shall see at the close of Topic 18.

But for the imperfect subjunctive a general rule of thumb may be established by remembering the present indicative/subjunctive verb usage following verbs of wishing, desiring, opinion, and so forth.

Voglio che tu *venga* a casa mia. *I want you to come to my house.* If **volere** appears *not* in the present but rather in a *simple* past, such as the imperfect indicative (**volevo**) or a *simple* conditional, **vorrei,** then the *imperfect subjunctive* must be used to maintain the proper sequence of events, or tense sequence.

Thus;

Voglio che tu *venga* a casa mia

in the past becomes:

Volevo che tu *venissi* a casa mia. (*I wanted you to come to my house.*)

And in the conditional, translated more literally:

Vorrei che tu *venissi* a casa mia. (*I would like that you might come to my house.*)

---

*An *etto* is one-tenth of a kilogram.

And:

Spera che voi *abbiate* ragione. (present indicative and subjunctive)

(*He hopes that you are right.*)

in the past becomes:

Sperava che voi *aveste* ragione. (*He hoped that you were right.*)

THE PLUPERFECT (TRAPASSATO)

The *pluperfect* is a compound tense formed by the combination of the imperfect of **avere** (for the most transitive verbs) or **essere** plus the past participle of the principal verb.

MODEL VERBS. Since the past participle in all the compound tenses is invariable except for the necessary agreement in gender, only the pluperfect tense for the *first* model verb, **parlare,** will be developed:

avevo parlato	I had spoken
avevi parlato	you had spoken
aveva parlato	he, she, you had spoken
avevamo parlato	we had spoken
avevate parlato	you had spoken
avevano parlato	they, you had spoken

With the verb **venire,** conjugated with **essere,** the pluperfect tense is formed thus:

ero venuto, a	I had come
eri venuto, a	you had come
era venuto, a	He, she, you had come
eravamo venuti, e	we had come
eravate venuti, e	you had come
erano venuti, e	they, you had come

USAGE. The pluperfect is used to express the English pluperfect ("I had spoken"; "I had come"; *had* being the indicative helping verb of the tense) and is also used to denote anterior action. Note the sequence of tenses:

Giorgio mi ha spedito l'articolo di cui *avevamo parlato. George mailed me the article we had talked about.*

This same usage, which is dependent upon the sequence of events and tense, is employed for the pluperfect subjunctive, again formed with the combination of the imperfect (subjunctive in this case!) and the past participle.

parlare	avessi parlato	avęssimo parlato
	avessi parlato	aveste parlato
	avesse parlato	avęssero parlato
venire	fossi venuto, a	fọssimo venuti, e
	fossi venuto, a	foste venuti, e
	fosse venuto, a	fọssero venuti, e

An explanation of the limitations and uses of this tense will be given under the "IF" CLAUSE heading in Topic 18.

THE PRETERIT; PROGRESSIVE TENSES; CONDITIONAL SENTENCES; *STARE*

THE PRETERIT

The *preterit,* or past absolute (or *passato remoto*—remote past) appears only in the indicative mood and expresses *one* action or state in the remote past.

FORMATION. The endings for the model verbs **parlare, vendere,** and **capire** are:

parlare	parl-*ai*	parl-*ammo*
	parl-*asti*	parl-*aste*
	parl-*ò*	parl-*arono*
vendere	vend-*ei*	vend-*emmo*
	vend-*esti*	vend-*este*
	vend-*è*	vend-*erono*
capire	cap-*ii*	cap-*immo*
	cap-*isti*	cap-*iste*
	cap-*ì*	cap-*irono*

Note that each conjugation, as in the imperfect tense, has the same set of endings except for the initial vowel of the ending, which is identical with the vowel of the infinitive termination: *a, e, i.* (The only exception to this useful key is the third person singular of the first conjugation: **parlare** becomes **parlò.**)

TRANSLATIONS. The preterit tense has two possible translations in English.

Parlai   *I spoke* AND *I did speak*

I spoke. Usually "I spoke" will be translated as the preterit tense. When one single action in the past is indicated, then the tense will usually be the preterit.

I did speak. The translation "I did speak" is the emphatic form of the preterit tense. The word "did" is of course not translated into Italian but serves as the key word to the use of the preterit tense in the sentence.

Actually, in conversational and modern Italian, the present perfect tense is preferred over the preterit tense. But the latter is used in historical narration and in literary style.

The *pluperfect* of the preterit is formed, as are all compound tenses, with the helping verbs **avere** or **ęssere** (this time in the preterit), plus the past participle. You should note the conjugations of the two helping verbs in the preterit.

avere	ebbi	avemmo	**ęssere**	fui	fummo
	avesti	aveste		fosti	foste
	ebbe	ębbero		fu	fųrono

As **avere** and **ęssere** are irregular, so other verbs may follow irregular conjugations in the preterit. Most will be recognizable though their stems might change. When in doubt consult a complete vocabulary or dictionary. For example:

prendere	(io) presi	(noi) prendemmo
	(tu) prendesti	(voi) prendeste
	(lui) prese	(loro) pręsero

VARIATION in the pluperfect tense is achieved by using the *preterit* tense of the auxiliary verbs **ęssere** or **avere** with the past participle. Nevertheless, there is no difference in the translation of the two tenses: both **avevo parlato** and **ebbi parlato** are translated as "I had spoken."

1. *Conditions.* The second pluperfect tense will be selected under these circumstances:

(a) The verb in the principal clause is in the preterit tense.

(b) The secondary clause is started with a conjunction of time such as **appena** or **appena che** (as soon as), **dopo che** (after), **quando** (when), and **sųbito che** (immediately after).

2. *Model verbs.* The second pluperfect tense thus becomes:

parlare	ebbi parlato	*I had spoken*
	avesti parlato	*you had spoken*
	ebbe parlato	*he, she, you had spoken*
	avemmo parlato	*we had spoken*
	aveste parlato	*you had spoken*
	ębbero parlato	*they, you had spoken*
venire	fui venuto/a	*I had come*
	fosti venuto/a	*you had come*
	fu venuto/a	*he, she, you had come*

fummo venuti/e   *we had come*
foste venuti/e   *you had come*
fụrono venuti/e   *they, you had come*

Dopo che fui partito, pranzạrono. (*After I had left, they dined.*)
Note. For the beginning student it might be helpful to consider
both the preterit and its pluperfect as recognition tenses only since
their conversational value is today greatly reduced.

PROGRESSIVE TENSES

Although the present and the imperfect tenses are usually employed
to translate the progressive actions, sometimes the present progressive and the past progressive tenses are substituted for more emphasis and for stylistic purposes.

Ascoltiamo (present), or Stiamo ascoltando (present progressive). *We are listening.*

THE PRESENT PROGRESSIVE TENSE is constructed by use of the
present tense of the verb **stare** and the present participle.

THE PAST PROGRESSIVE TENSE is constructed by use of the imperfect tense of the verb **stare** and the present participle.

Chiudẹvano (imperfect), or Stạvano chiudendo (past progressive). *They were closing.*

CONDITIONAL SENTENCES

THE "IF" CLAUSE. A true conditional sentence is characterized by
the word "if." In Italian, this condition is expressed in the present
indicative:

Se viene, si divertirà. *If she comes, she'll have a good time.*

Yet some conditional sentences may be "contrary to fact": that is,
they say something which is improbable or represents a hypothetical cause and effect. There is a strict sequence of tenses which must
be adhered to in the formation of these "contrary to fact" sentences. The rule is:

1. When the "if" clause is stated in the imperfect subjunctive, the
"result" clause must be in the simple conditional.

Se non *piovesse, farei* una passeggiata.* *If it weren't raining, I'd
go for a walk.*

*The "contrary to fact" aspect here is that it *is* raining!

2. When the "if" clause is stated in the pluperfect subjunctive (a compound tense), the "result" clause must be in the conditional perfect (a compound tense also).

Se non *fosse piovuto, avrei fatto* una passeggiata.* *If it hadn't rained, I would have taken a walk.*

Se non piove, faccio una passeggiata. *If it doesn't rain, I'll take a walk.*

Here are other examples.
1. (a) Se lo *conosci* bene, non *dirai* niente. (present/future) *If you know him well, you won't say anything.*
(b) Se lo *conoscessi* bene, non *diresti* niente. (imperfect subjunctive/conditional) *If you knew him well (and you don't), you wouldn't say anything.*
(c) Se lo *avessi conosciuto* bene, non *avresti detto* niente. (pluperfect subjunctive/past conditional) *If you had known him well, you wouldn't have said anything.*
2. Note another sequence usage:
(a) Benchè lo *sapessi* io, non *direi* niente. *Even though I knew it, I wouldn't say anything.*
(b) Benchè lo *avessi saputo,* non *avrei detto* niente. *Even though I might have known it, I wouldn't have said anything.*

STARE

One use of **stare** has been seen already in the illustration of the present and past progressive tenses. Here are two more uses:
1. **Stare** is employed in expressions of temporality and generality as in questions of health.

Come sta? Sto bene. *How are you? I am well.*
2. **Stare** is also employed to indicate temporary location or position and in certain idioms.

Sta a scuola. *He's at school.*

Stanno per comprare la cartolina. *They are about to buy the postcard.*

---

*This is contrary to fact in the past since, in the context of this sentence, it *did* rain and the subject *did not* take a walk. Compare this with the meaning expressed by the sentence in the present tense:

THE PASSIVE VOICE; SUFFIXES: AUGMENTATIVES AND DIMINUTIVES; VERBALS: ADDITION AND REVIEW; FARE AND VEDERE + INFINITIVE; INDEFINITE PRONOUNS

THE PASSIVE VOICE

The passive voice is best understood by first defining "active voice." Simply stated, the *active* voice is used when the subject of the sentence does the action. The *passive* voice is used when the subject of the sentence is acted upon or receives the action of the sentence.

Il professore *scrisse* il primo capitolo di questo volume. (active) *The professor wrote the first chapter of this volume.*

Il primo capitolo di questo volume *fu scritto* dal professore. (passive) *The first chapter of this volume was written by the professor.* From this example you can see that the *pure* passive form is constructed in Italian in the various tenses by the use of **essere** plus the past participle of the principal verb—**fu scritto.**

Il pane *è portato* a casa. *The bread is brought home.*

Le studentesse *sono state passate. The female students have been passed.*

OTHER FORMS.

1. The more idiomatic and preferred Italian way of expressing the passive voice is, as we have already seen, with the reflexive form of the verb.

instead of Italiano *è parlato* in questo paese.

preferred Si parla italiano in questo paese. *Italian is spoken/One speaks Italian in this country.*

2. Another form of the passive, far less frequently used, is the use of **stare** plus the past participle.

La porta *sta chiusa. The door is closed.*

To convey emotion, **rimanere** is also employed.

Quando si è partita io sono rimasto male. *When she left I was upset.*

3. **Venire** sometimes replaces ẹssere (plus past participle) to express a more active form.

Il conto *è pagato* ogni mese. *The bill is paid every month.*

Il conto *viene pagato* ogni mese. *The bill gets paid every month.*

AND

Lo sportello *era aperto*. *The window was open.* (state of being)

Lo sportello *venne aperto*. *The window was opened.* (active state)

4. Occasionally **andare** plus the past participle is used to show obligation.

Questi soldi non *vanno messi* in qualsịasi posto. *This money shouldn't be put just anywhere.*

SUFFIXES: AUGMENTATIVES AND DIMINUTIVES
(suffissi apprezzativi)

Instead of using an adjective like **grande** (big), **pịccolo** (little), or **cattivo** (bad), the native Italian speaker usually prefers to add a suffix to the noun, often showing endearment or humor. Those suffixes which denote "bigness," implying "grande," follow.

AUGMENTATIVES. The most widely used suffix among the augmentatives is -*one.*

un libro—un libr*one*   *a big book*

In words that employ different endings for the masculine and the feminine, -*ona* is used exclusively for the feminine.

la ragazza—la ragazz*ona*   *the big girl*

il ragazzo—il ragazz*one*   *the big boy*

It should be noted also that the suffix -*one* will often change the gender of a noun. For example, **una donna**—**un donnone** (a big woman).

Also, -*otto,* an augmentative, often means strong and young: **un ragazzotto** (a strong young man). It may also indicate some animals' young: **tigre** (tiger)—**tigrotto** (cub).

DIMINUTIVES. Many diminutive suffixes exist for expressing "smallness" (**pịccolo**) and endearment and even sympathy: for example, -*ino, -etto, -ello.* However, the student should be cautious in the construction of the noun plus suffix combination, remembering that the diminutive forms are *not* interchangeable and are often applicable only to given forms.

ʹragazzo il ragazz*ino* il ragazz*etto* (*the little boy*)
BUT il fratello il fratell*ino* NOT fratell*etto*
(*little brother*)

Clearly, certain nouns will tolerate only certain diminutive suffixes.

lo zio	lo zi*etto* (NOT ziino)	*cute uncle*
il cugino	il cugin*etto*	*little cousin*
bene	ben*ino*	*quite good*
il vento	il vent*icello*	*breeze*
la mano	la man*ina*	*pretty little hand*

And note the irregular formation of **il cane—il cagnolino** and **magro—magrolino**.

OTHER SPECIAL USES.
1. The diminutive *-uccia* sometimes carries a *derogatory* meaning.
la casa—la cas*uccia* *the poor, untidy house*
2. The ending *-accio* at times can mean *evil*.
la parola—la parol*accia* *curse word*
3. The suffix *-astro* usually means *false*.
il poeta—il poet*astro* *poetaster*
4. The diminutive *-astro* can also indicate *kinship*.
sorella—sorell*astra* *half-sister*

VERBALS: ADDITION AND REVIEW

The following verbal patterns may be difficult and thus need review for mastery.
1. When an article of clothing or a part of the body is involved in a verbal expression, the reflexive verb should be used to show possession with the definite article preceding the noun.

Giovanni si è lavato le mani. *John has washed his hands.*

Gina e Maria si sono pettinate i capelli. *Gina and Mary have combed their hair.*

In questa stagione Enrico si mette sempre il cappello. *In this season Henry always puts on his hat.*

Note. Don't confuse the similar construction used by the Italian:

Mi lavano i piatti. *They are washing* my *dishes.*

2. Adverbs such as **appena** (just), **già** (already), and **mai** (never) often split the two components of compound verbs. Note the translation of the following phrases.

È appena entrato. *He has just come in.*

Abbiamo *già* letto questo passo? *Have we already read this passage?*

Non l'ho *mai* letto.* *I've never read it.*

*Remember that verbs requiring **avere** as a helping verb will agree in the past participle with the direct object **only** when the direct object pronoun precedes the verb.

Hai letto gli artịcoli? *Have you read the articles?*

Sì, li ho lett*i*.

3. The past participle of verbs requiring ẹssere (including reflexive verbs) agrees with the subject of the verb.

Giovanna è andata a casa sua. *Jean has gone to her house.*

4. After the prepositions **senza** and **dopo,** the infinitive is often used.

Andò avanti senza *aspettarmi*. *He went on ahead without waiting for me.*

Dopo *aver spedito* il pacchetto, fece una passeggiata. *After having mailed the package, she took a walk.*

The above example is similar in usage to the absolute construction in the following:

Fatt*i* i cọmpiti per domani, si mise a mangiare. *Having done tomorrow's homework, he started eating.*

5. Notice the distinctions between similar expressions such as **avere bisogno di** (to need something) and **bisognare** (it is necessary) and **avere voglia di** (to feel like) and **volere** (to want).

Abbiamo bisogno della carta. *We need the menu.*

Bisogna vedere prima una carta. *It is first necessary to see a menu.*

AND

Ho voglia di fare una passeggiata. *I feel like taking a walk.*

Vorrei fare una passeggiata. *I would like to take a walk.*

FARE AND VEDERE + INFINITIVE

1. **Fare** plus the infinitive means "to have something done (by someone else)." Note the distinctions:

Mi fece andare. *He made me go.*

Ho fatto costruire questa casa. *I had this house built.*

But:

Gli ho fatto costruire questa casa. *I had* him *build this house.*

Lui sa far fare tutto. *He knows how to get everything done.*

2. **Vedere** functions like **fare** when the object is a pronoun.

L'ha vista venire. *He saw her coming.*

Or even:

Gliene vedo comprare spesso. *I see him buying some often.*

But when nouns are expressed:

Ha visto venire Giovanna. *He saw Giovanna coming.*

and:

Vedo Angelo comprarne spesso. *I see Angelo buying some often.*

INDEFINITE PRONOUNS

Most indefinite pronouns are used in the singular and are not further declined. (Note the exceptions* in the following list.) The most common forms are:

altro/a/i/e*	*other, another*
certuno	*a certain (person)*
chiunque	*whoever*
ciascuno	*each one*
molto/a/i/e*	*much, many*
nessuno	*no one, nobody*
niente	*nothing*
nulla	*nothing*
nullo	*none, no one*
ogni	*each, every*
ognuno	*each one, every one*
parecchio/a/i/e*	*several, a great deal of*
poco/a, pochi, poche*	*a few*
qualche	*any, some*
qualcheduno	*anybody, somebody*
qualcuno	*someone, somebody*
qualunque	*any, whatever*
taluno	*such a one*
troppo/a/i/e*	*too much, too many*
tutto/a/i/e*	*all*
tutto	*the entire*
un poco di, or, un po' di	*a little of*
un certo	*a certain one*
uno	*one*

IRREGULAR VERBS; ORTHOGRAPHIC CHANGES IN VERBS; ABBREVIATED PATTERNS FOR IRREGULARS

Some rules for irregular verbs can be devised, but the best general principle is that the verbal forms should be absorbed by the student slowly, but constantly. It is merely a pedagogical exercise to list all the ramifications of all the irregular verbs under a set of rules which takes longer to memorize than the irregular forms themselves. The following summary of some of the most useful guides should be studied in conjunction with the list of the principal irregular verbs at the book's end.

REGULAR FORMS. Note that not all forms of an irregular verb are irregular. For example, if one excludes essere, irregular verbs have regular endings for these forms:
1. Present participle.
2. Second person plural of the present indicative.
3. Imperfect tense.
4. Second person singular and first and second persons plural of the preterit tense.
5. Imperfect subjunctive tense.

IRREGULAR VERBS, BY CONJUGATION

The *first* conjugation has only four irregular verbs:
  *fare, *andare, *dare, and ***stare.**

A brief guide to some of these verbs' irregular principal parts has been provided at the end of this Topic (see Abbreviated Patterns for Irregular Verbs). However, when in doubt, principal parts of irregular verbs should always be checked in a reliable dictionary.

The *second* conjugation may be divided into three groups. The most convenient procedure is to learn the model verb for each group. As one studies the other irregular verbs, one can associate each new verb with the model verb as a guide.

VERBS ENDING IN *-RE* AND *-RRE.* The principal verbs are:

*bere (bevere)	*to drink*
*dire	*to say, to tell*
porre	*to put, to place*
tradurre	*to translate*
trarre	*to pull*

All compounds of these verbs will follow the main pattern: for example, **benedire** (to bless) or **imporre** (to impose).

VERBS WITH STRESS ON THE NEXT-TO-THE-LAST SYLLABLE. The principal verbs are:

cadere	*to fall*
dolere	*to pain*
*dovere	*must, ought* (to have to —expressing obligation)
godere	*to enjoy*
parere	*to appear, to seem*
persuadere	*to persuade*
*piacere	*to be pleasing*
*potere	*can, to be able*
rimanere	*to stay, remain*
*sapere	*to know*
*sedere	*to sit*
tenere	*to hold, to have*
valere	*to be worth*
*vedere	*to see*
*volere	*to wish, to want*

VERBS WITH THE STRESS ON THE SYLLABLE BEFORE the next-to-the-last syllable. The list of these irregular verbs is by far the longest, but one should observe that many of these verbs are not used frequently.

affigere	*to affix*
ardere	*to burn*
assistere	*to assist, to attend*
assumere	*to assume*
chiedere	*to ask*
*chiudere	*to shut*

*Contained in List of Irregular verbs at the end of this book.

cogliere	to gather
concedere	to concede
*conoscere	to know
correre	to run
crescere	to grow
cuocere	to cook
dirigere	to direct
discutere	to discuss
distinguere	to distinguish
*leggere	to read
*mettere	to put, to place
mordere	to bite
muovere	to move
nascere	to be born
perdere	to lose
piangere	to weep
porgere	to hand over
*prendere	to take
ridere	to laugh
*rispondere	to answer
rompere	to break
scegliere	to choose
*scrivere	to write
spargere	to spread
spegnere	to extinguish
spendere	to spend
vincere	to win
*vivere	to live
volgere	to turn

The *third* conjugation has only a few irregular verbs (with of course their compounds):

apparire	to appear
aprire	to open
assalire	to assail
coprire	to cover
cucire	to sew
morire	to die

*Contained in List of Irregular verbs at the end of this book.

offrire	*to offer*
partire	*to leave*
salire	*to go up*
udire	*to hear*
uscire	*to go out*
*venire	*to come*

ORTHOGRAPHIC CHANGES IN VERBS

These changes in verb form are essentially not irregular because there are certain rules which govern the addition or omission of a letter. One guiding principle, not always valid (as is unfortunately so often the case), is that the spelling change is made to preserve as closely as possible the original sound: that is, the sound found in the infinitive.

FIRST CONJUGATION CHANGES

1. Verbs that end in *-care* and *-gare* add the letter *h* when the *c* and *g* is followed by an *e* or *i*.

dimenticare *to forget* and pregare *to pray*

2. Verbs that end in *-ciare* and *-giare* omit the *i* before *e* or *i* because it is superfluous.

cominciare *to begin*   mangiare *to eat*

3. Some verbs that end in *-iare* maintain the *i*, if it is *stressed*, even before another *i*.

avviare *to give a start*.

The present indicative of this verb is:

avvịo	avviamo
avvịi	avviate
avvịa	avvịano

4. Some verbs that end in *-iare* lose the *i* when unstressed before another *i*.

studiare   *to study*.

The present indicative of this verb is:

studio	studiamo
studi	studiate
studia	stụdiano

*Contained in List of Irregular verbs at the end of this book.

SECOND CONJUGATION CHANGES: A few verbs that end in *-cere* and *-gere* place the letter *i* before the past participle ending *-uto.*

piacere   *to be pleasing—piaciuto*

IDIOMS

To attempt to give a list of common Italian idioms would be unrealistic. A language is, in itself, idiomatic when we think about the very meaning of the word *idiom:* "peculiarity," "specific property," "unique feature." It is this uniqueness that ultimately distinguishes one language from another in allowing certain "peculiarities" to remain outside logical grammatical analysis.

The *idiom* is different from the *locuzione* ("expression") in that the idiom substitutes for a grammatical form simply not found in the target language. A *locuzione* is a formulated expression that may rely on historical or sociological rationales. For example, the common telephone introduction of "Hi! It's me, Frank" (or, more purely grammatical: "It's I") rendered in Italian idiom is **"Ciao! Sono io, Franco."**

Likewise, phrases such as "to be right" and "to agree with" must be translated idiomatically as: **avere ragione** and **dare ragione a (una persona).**

An example of a *locuzione* might be:

Quella mi *fa gli occhi di triglia.*

(Literally: *That one is making mullet eyes at me.*)

Yet unless rendered into our own idiomatic (unique) pattern (probably something like: "She's making goo-goo eyes at me"), the expression is a baffling image!

Many idioms include the common verbs **avere** and **fare** (see Weather Expressions—**fa bel tempo,** etc.). You should be aware of the formation of idioms using these two verbs as well as with the verb **dare.**

Non facciamo tardi. *Let's not be late.*

Faccio una doccia. *I'm taking a shower.*

ABBREVIATED PATTERNS FOR IRREGULARS

Arranged by conjugation, these verb parts will follow the infinitive form for each verb: *present indicative* (complete conjugation given only when necessary); first three persons of the *preterit;* the *past participle;* and the first person of the *present subjunctive.*

THE SECOND CONJUGATION:

1. **porre:** pongo, poni, pone, etc; posi, ponesti, pose; posto; ponga.

   tradurre: traduco, traduci, traduce, etc.; tradussi, traducesti, tradusse; tradotto; traduca.

   trarre: traggo, trai, trae, traiamo, traete, traggono; trassi, traesti, trasse; tratto; tragga.

2. **dolere:** dolgo, duoli, duole, doliamo, dolete, dolgono; dolsi, dolesti, dolse; doluto; dolga.

   parere: paio, pari, pare, paiamo, parete, paiono; parvi, paresti, parve; parso; paia.

   rimanere: rimango, rimani, rimane, etc.; rimasi, rimanesti, rimase; rimasto; rimanga.

   tenere: tengo, tieni, tiene, teniamo, tenete, tengono; tenni, tenesti, tenne; tenuto; tenga.

3. **chiudere:** chiudo, chiudi, etc.; chiusi, chiudesti, chiuse; chiuso; chiuda.

   correre: corro, corri, etc.; corsi, corresti, corse; corso; corra.

   dirigere: dirigo, dirigi, etc.; diressi, dirigesti, diresse; diretto; diriga.

   muovere: muovo, muovi, muove, moviamo, movete, muovono; mossi, movesti, mosse; mosso; muova.

   nascere: nasco, nasci, etc.; nacqui, nascesti, nacque; nato; nasca.

   perdere: perdo, perdi, etc.; persi, perdesti, perse; perso; perda.

   ridere: rido, ridi, etc.; risi, ridesti, rise; riso; rida.

   rompere: rompo, rompi, etc.; ruppi, rompesti, ruppe; rotto; rompa.

   scegliere: scelgo, scegli, sceglie, etc.; scelsi, scegliesti, scelse; scelto; scelga.

   spegnere: spengo, spegni, spegne, etc.; spensi, spegnesti, spense; spento; spenga.

   spendere: spendo, spendi, etc.; spesi, spendesti, spese; speso; spenda.

   vincere: vinco, vinci, etc.; vinsi, vincesti, vinse; vinto; vinca.

   volgere: volgo, volgi, etc.; volsi, volgesti, volse; volto; volga.

THE THIRD CONJUGATION:

apparire: same endings as **parere** above.

aprire: apro, apri, etc.; apersi, apristi, aperse; aperto; apra.

morire: muoio, muori, muore, moriamo, morite, muoiono; morii, moristi, morì; morto; muoia.

offrire: offro, offri, etc.; offersi, offristi, offerse; offerto; offra.

udire: odo, odi, ode, udiamo, udite, ọdono; udii, udisti, udì; udito; oda.

uscire: esco, esci, esce, usciamo, uscite, ẹscono; uscii, uscisti, uscì; uscito; esca.

REVIEW EXERCISES, TOPICS 17–20

PATTERN DRILLS. Conjugate the infinitives in the indicative mood in the present, imperfect, conditional, and past conditional, responding with the infinitives which require the subjunctive in the respective tenses: present, imperfect, and pluperfect subjunctive.

1. Io (volere) che noi (sbrigarsi).
2. Maria (pensare) che lei (dovere) rispọndere.
3. Io (temere) che lui non (potere) vedere Roma.
4. Noi (sperare) che loro (dare) l'indirizzo.
5. Se non (nevicare), noi (andare) a mangiare fuori.

TRANSLATE the following sentences into Italian.

1. If they come back, they will not find us.
2. These documents will not be sold by his nephew.
3. We want them to come, don't we?
4. If the teacher had not explained the poem, he would not have understood it.
5. It has just rained, hasn't it?
6. The girls washed their hands.
7. They are unhappy that the guests cannot come.
8. I do not know anyone who lives nearby.
9. Do not close that door, please.
10. The newspapers are sold everywhere.
11. Although he is rich, he is not very happy.
12. We have the best car that I've ever seen.
13. John is speaking very slowly so that the Americans may understand him.
14. They have just gone to eat at Maria's, but she has a headache.
15. I saw the book you (pl.) had talked about.
16. Why did you get up so late?
17. I had already read it when he asked me to buy him a copy.
18. I had him do it.
19. I was wanting you to come with me.

20. They saw her arrive.
21. Only new books are sold here.
22. I was right! He sold me that car five years ago.
23. I would have gone if they had told me about it.
24. While you (pl.) were reading, the phone rang.
25. My little brother always asks me the same thing.
26. They were about to eat when we arrived.
27. Years ago, he had a new bedroom built without realizing the money he was spending.
28. Each one did as he wished.
29. If I were a millionaire, I wouldn't know how to amuse myself.
30. After having read every work (of it), I decided to translate the entire works.

TRANSLATE this brief tale:

Quando un certo povero vecchio (*old man*) decise che non poteva più sopportare (*stand*) la fame, prese un pezzo di pane che aveva da un bel pezzo (*for a good long time*) e andò a tenere il pane sopra il fumo del fuoco di un certo cuoco (*cook*). Arrabbiato il cuoco lo mandò da un giudice per pagare il fumo al cuoco. La condanna (*sentence*)? Il cuoco andrebbe pagato con il suono di una moneta battuta (from *battere*) su un tavolo.

COMPOSE A BRIEF SENTENCE using the forms of the irregular verbs supplied:
1. offrire (1st person singular, present perfect indicative)
2. rompere (3rd person singular, present perfect indicative)
3. salire (3rd person plural, present subjunctive)
4. tradurre (3rd person plural, present indicative)
5. rimanere (1st person singular, present indicative)
6. vincere (2nd person singular, present perfect subjunctive)
7. scegliere (3rd person plural, imperfect subjunctive)
8. chiudere (1st person plural, present perfect indicative)
9. leggere (3rd person singular, preterit indicative)
10. potere (2nd person singular, present subjunctive)

READING AND TRANSLATION

READING. The student is now ready for the reading and translation of material in Italian, if s/he has not already been doing this. Of course, the reading of great works from Italian literature, such as the *Promessi Sposi* by Manzoni or even Dante's *Divina Commedia,* represents the highest aim and achievement of serious mastery of the Italian language. However, before these efforts can be undertaken, the student should begin to read easy, contemporary Italian prose. By no means, however, does this imply insipid material, nor does it mean material which is edited for the English-speaking reader.

TRANSLATION. The following passage from *La storia di Firenze* discusses details of the physical and social "face lift" which resulted when Florence (*Firenze*) became, briefly, the capital of the then newly formed monarchy of Italy (1865).

READING PROCESS. The process outlined below will lead to reading fluency that will allow the student greater comprehension and reading speed and a richer vocabulary:

Step 1. First Reading. Read the passage out loud and slowly. Try to visualize what the text is saying, even if you have to guess at the meaning of some of the words. DO NOT TRANSLATE word for word, looking up every word you do not immediately know. Try to understand what the text is expressing the first time you read it. This is the skill you want ultimately to perfect.

Step 2. Text Word List. Read the passage aloud again, thought pattern by thought pattern. On a separate sheet of paper (not in the margin!) make a list of forms and phrases you do not understand.

Step 3. Word List and Dictionary. Leave the text and look up the words or phrases on your list. The following Word-Phrase List, arranged by line number, should help you.

WORD-PHRASE LIST
Line   *Words or Phrases*
1   *abitanti*—inhabitants

2   *accogliere*—to welcome/to accommodate; *circa*—about

3   *in maggioranza*—mostly; *costituire*—to constitute; *personale*—personnel

4   *divenuto*—(which had) become; *regno*—reign; *abbastanza*—enough; *sistemare*—to situate

5   *pubblici*—public; *fabbricati*—buildings

6   *ricchezza*—wealth; *uomini d'affari*—businessmen; *fine Medioevo*—end (of) the Middle Ages; *aveva moltiplicato*—(subject of this verb is *ricchezza*) had multiplied

7   *palazzi*—palaces; *alloggio*—lodging; *pose*—(preterit of *porre*)

8   *fino ad allora*—until then

9   *pressochè*—almost; *territorio*—territory (subject of *era stato*-8); *cinta*—wall; *primi*—(*abitanti* understood)

10   *secolo*—century; *architetto*—architect

11   *disciplinare*—to regulate; *espansione*—expansion; *sarebbe potuta riuscire*—could have been able to turn out

12   *attuare/-uando*—(gerund) carrying out

13   *permettere a*—to allow; *legarsi*—to link itself; *armoniosamente*—harmoniously; *zona*—zone

14   *fuori di*—outside; *mura*—(plural of *muro*) here meaning city walls; *assorbire*—to absorb; *dilatandosi*—(gerund ending with *si*—reflexive!); *dilatarsi*—to expand

15   *da*—from; *quadrati*—square; *abbattere*—to knock down

16   *riva*—bank; *le*—them; *sostituire*—to substitute; *viali*—avenues; *alberati*—tree-lined

17   *tagliati*—(past participle of *tagliare*) cut; *simmetriche*—symmetrical; *aree*—(plural of *area,* equal to English cognate); *porte*—here meaning gates; *fa sistemare*—(*fare* + infinitive—to have something done)

18   *Piazzale*—a large *piazza; belvedere*—a beautiful view

19   *passeggiata*—walk; *vi*—there; *condurre*—to lead; *all'interno*—inside

20   *allargare*—to widen; *vie*—streets; *principali*—main

21   *occupata*—(same as English cognate); *successivamente*—subsequently; *foro*—forum

22   *mercato*—market; *medievale*—Medieval; *inoltre*—also; *movimento*—movement

23   *da*—for; *faceva*—(had made); *di*—of

24   *s'intensifica/intensificarsi*—to intensify; *per via*—by means of; *organi governativi*—government offices

25.   *stampa*—press (newspapers); *fila*—line; *fondare*—to found
26   *moltiplicarsi*—(repeated again!);   *abbondare*—to abound;
       periodici—periodicals; *letterari*—literary

Step 4. Text and Word List. Consulting your word list, read the
passage out loud again, thought pattern by thought pattern, until
you can visualize what is being expressed. If the passage is not
relatively clear, check your list for a mistaken meaning.

The Passage: Firenze Capitale del Regno d'Italia

Firenze aveva centodiecimila abitanti nel milleottocento-
cinquantuno. Essa doveva accogliere circa trentamila persone
3 in maggioranza piemontesi che costituivano il personale di
Sardegna divenuto regno d'Italia. Fu abbastanza facile sistemare
i servizi pubblici nei fabbricati di un'antica capitale nella
6 quale la ricchezza degli uomini d'affari di fine Medioevo aveva
moltiplicato gl'immensi palazzi. Ma l'alloggio delle persone pose
gravi problemi alla città alla quale fino ad allora era stato
9 pressochè sufficiente il territorio dentro la cinta dei primi del
quattordicesimo secolo. Un architetto di gran talento, Giuseppe
Poggi, seppe disciplinare un'espansione che sarebbe potuta riuscire
12 catastrofica, attuando un progetto che aveva preparato. Per
permettere alla città di legarsi armoniosamente alla zona di tre
chilometri fuori delle mura che sta assorbendo, dilatandosi così
15 da sei a quarantaquattro chilometri quadrati, egli abbatte le mura
della riva destra e le sostituisce con dei larghi viali alberati,
tagliati da piazze simmetriche sulle aree delle antiche porte; fa
18 sistemare il Piazzale Michelangelo, belvedere sopra la città e la
magnifica passeggiata che vi conduce; all'interno della città
allarga le vie principali e apre una grande piazza centrale sull'area
21 che era stata occupata successivamente dal foro romano e dall'antico
mercato medievale. Inoltre, il movimento intellettuale e artistico
che da venti anni faceva di Firenze il centro spirituale della nuova
24 Italia s'intensifica per via della presenza degli organi governativi.
La stampa, con in prima fila "La Nazione", fondata nel milleottocento-
sessantuno, si moltiplica mentre abbondano i periodici letterari e
27 politici.

Step 5. Translation. Attempt a rough translation of the text. It
should look something like this.

Florence, Capital of the Reign of Italy

Florence had one hundred ten thousand inhabitants in 1851. It had
to accommodate about thirty thousand people, mostly people from

the region of the Piedmont who constituted the personnel of Sardinia which had become the reign of Italy. It was easy enough to situate the public services in the buildings of an ancient capital in which the wealth of the businessmen of the end of the Middle Ages had multiplied the immense palaces. But the lodging of the people posed grave problems to (for) the city (for) which until then it had almost been sufficient the territory inside the wall of the first inhabitants of the fourteenth century. A very talented architect, Joseph Poggi, knew how to regulate an expansion that could have been able to turn out (to be) catastrophic, carrying out a project that he had prepared; in order to allow the city to link itself harmoniously to the zone of three kilometers outside the walls that it was absorbing, expanding thus from six to forty-four kilometers square, he (Poggi) knocks down the walls of the right bank and substitutes them with some wide, tree-lined avenues, cut from symmetrical plazas around the areas of the ancient (city) gates. He has Michelangelo Square situated (set up) as a beautiful viewpoint above the city and the magnificent walk that leads there. Inside the city he widens the main thoroughfares and opens a large, central plaza (square) in the area that had been occupied before by the Roman forum and the old medieval market. Also, the intellectual and artistic movement, which for twenty years had made out of Florence the spiritual center of the new Italy, intensifies by means of the presence of the government offices. The press, with the newspaper *The Nation* in the front line, founded in 1861, expands while literary and political periodicals abound.

Step 6. Revised Text. Now that you have a clear understanding of the text, revise your rough version of the passage into a smooth English rendition.

Step 7. Review. Reread the text and enjoy your mastery of the meaning and the sounds of the Italian passage. Then, the first few times, return to your two translations to see how your understanding of the text became more precise.

FLORENCE: THE FIRST CAPITAL OF THE ITALIAN MONARCHY

In 1851, Florence had 110,000 inhabitants. It soon had to accommodate close to 30,000 more, mostly those from the Piedmont, who constituted the personnel from the Sardinian government, which had become the Italian Monarchy. It was easy enough to situate the public services in the buildings of an old capital city where the wealth of late medieval businessmen had multiplied the immense palaces of the commercial center. But the lodging of that many people posed serious problems for the city which, until then, had sufficed with the land inside the walls of its fourteenth-century forefathers. Joseph Poggi, a superb architect, knew how to regulate an expansion that could have turned out to be catastrophic, carrying out a project he had designed. To allow the city to join gracefully the three-kilometer tract it was absorbing outside its walls, expanding from six to forty-four square kilometers, Poggi knocks down the walls along the right bank and replaces them with wide, tree-lined avenues, which stem from symmetrical plazas around the ancient gates of the city. He establishes Michelangelo Square as a panoramic viewpoint above the city and the magnificent avenue that leads there. Within the city he widens the main thoroughfares and opens up a large, central square where there had previously stood the Roman forum and the old medieval market. Also, the intellectual and artistic movement, which over the last twenty years had been establishing Florence as the spiritual center of the new Italy, grows through the presence of the new government offices. The press, with the newspaper *The Nation* in the front line with its founding in 1861, expands while literary and political periodicals abound.

The student should also have practice in "nontranslation" exercise, that is to say, in reading an Italian text for comprehension and information. The process outlined as follows will ultimately lead to a reading fluency that will allow the student a certain independence from the two-stage translation process.

Step 1. Text. Read the passage out loud. Try to visualize what the text is saying, even if you have to guess at the meaning of some vocabulary. DO NOT TRANSLATE. Try to understand what the text is expressing the first time you read it. This is the skill you want ultimately to perfect.

Step 2. Text plus Word List. Read the passage aloud again, thought pattern (or sentence) by thought pattern. On a separate sheet of paper (NOT IN THE MARGIN) make a list of forms and phrases you do not understand.

Step 3. Word List and Dictionary. Leave the text and look up the words or phrases on your list.

Step 4. Text and Word List. Consulting your word list, read the passage out loud again, thought pattern by thought pattern, until you can visualize what is being expressed. DO NOT TRANSLATE. The text should make sense in Italian. If there are problems, check your list for a mistaken phrase or meaning.

Step 5. Text. Be sure you understand the passage, then read it again aloud. Concentrate on reading aloud in such a way as to emphasize the meaning of the text. If you find it helps, lightly mark the stress patterns and the phrase groupings with a pencil.

Step 6. Review. Reread the text and enjoy your mastery of the meaning and the sounds of the passage.

ANSWERS TO REVIEW EXERCISES, TOPICS 2–7

PATTERN DRILLS

1. Non parliamo inglese.
   Non parlano inglese.
   Non parla inglese.
   Non parlo inglese.
   Non parlate inglese.
   Non parli inglese.

2. Studiamo quelle lezioni a casa.
   Studiano quelle lezioni a casa.
   Studia quelle lezioni a casa.
   Studio quelle lezioni a casa.
   Studiate quelle lezioni a casa.
   Studi quelle lezioni a casa.

3. Ripetiamo le parole lunghe.
   Ripetono le parole lunghe.
   Ripete le parole lunghe.
   Ripeto le parole lunghe.
   Ripetete le parole lunghe.
   Ripeti le parole lunghe.

4. Ascoltiamo ora.
   Ascoltano ora.
   Ascolta ora.
   Ascolto ora.
   Ascoltate ora.
   Ascolti ora.

5. Abbiamo il libro di Marta.
   Hanno il libro di Marta.

    Ha il libro di Marta.
    Ho il libro di Marta.
    Avete il libro di Marta.
    Hai il libro di Marta.
6. Capiamo molto bene.
    Capiscono molto bene.
    Capisce molto bene.
    Capisco molto bene.
    Capite molto bene.
    Capisci molto bene.
7. Non siamo in Italia, siamo in Svizzera.
    Non sono in Italia, sono in Svizzera.
    Non è in Italia, è in Svizzera.
    Non sono in Italia, sono in Svizzera.
    Non siete in Italia, siete in Svizzera.
    Non sei in Italia, sei in Svizzera.
8. Andiamo a Firenze.
    Vanno a Firenze.
    Va a Firenze.
    Vado a Firenze.
    Andate a Firenze.
    Vai a Firenze.
9. Non sappiamo niente.
    Non sanno niente.
    Non sa niente.
    Non so niente.
    Non sapete niente.
    Non sai niente.
10. Diciamo la verità.
    Dicono la verità.
    Dice la verità.
    Dico la verità.
    Dite la verità.
    Dici la verità.

TRANSLATION
1. Giovanni non legge mai le lezioni d'italiano.
2. Buon giorno, Signorina Bolaffi. Come sta?
3. Vai all'università oggi?
4. Non studiamo l'italiano oggi nè domani.
5. Lui ascolta il professore e capisce tutto.

6. Perchè arriva a scuola presto?
7. Il signor Buoncore è un buon professore.
8. Fate tutte le lezioni, non è vero?
9. Partiamo presto per Roma?
10. Quando arriva a casa?
11. Preferiscono l'automobile di Giuseppe. È molto bella.
12. Ecco il *medico*! Corre.
13. Tu sai tutto.
14. Beve l'acqua?
15. Andiamo al museo.

TRANSLATION AND PLURAL

1. Il ragazzo finisce questo libro.
   I ragazzi finiscono questi libri.
2. Capisce la ragazza quelle lezioni?
   Capiscono le ragazze quelle lezioni?
3. La città francese è bella.
   Le città francesi sono belle.
4. Lui ascolta il professore d'italiano.
   Ascoltano i professori d'italiano.
5. Non sono all'università; è lei che frequenta quell'università.
   Non siamo all'università; sono loro che frequentano quelle
   università.
6. Vado a casa per fare il mio compito.
   Andiamo a casa per fare i nostri compiti.
7. Suo fratello ha la mia matita.
   I loro fratelli hanno le nostre matite.
8. Lui sa il compito.
   Loro sanno i compiti.
9. Andiamo a Arezzo per vedere le chiese.
   Vado a Arezzo per vedere la chiesa.
10. Fanno belle scatole azzurre.
    Fa una bella scatola azzurra.

PREPOSIZIONI ARTICOLATE

1. (di) della dello delle dei   dell'
2. (su) sulla sul   sui   sull' sulla
3. (da) dal   dallo dagli dal
4. (in) nel   nella nel   negli nei
5. (a)   agli   alle   alla   al
6. (con) col   col   con   coll'

ANSWERS TO REVIEW EXERCISES, TOPICS 8–11

PATTERN DRILLS

1. Il professore non *viene* in classe.
   Il professore non *è venuto* in classe.
   Il professore non *verrà* in classe.
   Il professore non *sarà venuto* in classe.
   Il professore non *verrebbe* in classe.
   Il professore non *sarebbe venuto* in classe.

2. Oggi tutti *si divertono* molto.
   Oggi tutti *si sono divertiti* molto.
   Oggi tutti *si divertiranno* molto.
   Oggi tutti *si saranno divertiti* molto.
   Oggi tutti *si divertirebbero* molto.
   Oggi tutti *si sarebbero divertiti* molto.

3. Quando *può* leggere il mio giornale?
   Quando *ha potuto* leggere il mio giornale?
   Quando *potrà* leggere il mio giornale?
   Quando *avrà potuto* leggere il mio giornale?
   Quando *potrebbe* leggere il mio giornale?
   Quando *avrebbe potuto* leggere il mio giornale?

4. *Conosciamo* a poco a poco la nuova studentessa francese.
   Abbiamo conosciuto a poco a poco la nuova studentessa francese.
   Conosceremo a poco a poco la nuova studentessa francese.
   Avremo conosciuto a poco a poco la nuova studentessa francese.
   Conosceremmo a poco a poco la nuova studentessa francese.
   Avremmo conosciuto a poco a poco la nuova studentessa francese.

5. *Volete* rimanere a casa?
   Siete voluti rimanere a casa?
   Vorrete rimanere a casa?
   Sarete voluti rimanere a casa?
   Vorreste rimanere a casa?
   Sareste voluti rimanere a casa?

6. *Continuo* a tenere a mente la poesia latina.
   Ho continuato a tenere a mente la poesia latina.

Continuerò a tenere a mente la poesia latina.

Avrò continuato a tenere a mente la poesia latina.

Continuerei a tenere a mente la poesia latina.

Avrei continuato a tenere a mente la posia latina.

7. Lo studente inglese *deve* parlare tedesco.

Lo studente inglese *ha dovuto* parlare tedesco.

Lo studente inglese *dovrò* parlare tedesco.

Lo studente inglese *avrà dovuto* parlare tedesco.

Lo studente inglese *dovrebbe* parlare tedesco.

Lo studente inglese *avrebbe dovuto* parlare tedesco.

8. *Prendiamo* il treno che *parte* alle otto e dieci.

Abbiamo preso il treno che *è partito* alle otto e dieci.

Prenderemo il treno che *partirà* alle otto e dieci.

Avremo preso il treno che *sarà partito* alle otto e dieci.

Prenderemmo il treno che *partirebbe* alle otto e dieci.

Avremmo preso il treno che *sarebbe partito* alle otto e dieci.

TRANSLATE

1. Che ore sono? Sono le cinque e mezza di mattina . . . più o meno.

2. Dove sono i libri italiani? Glieli daremo.

3. Queste case dipinte di azzurro e di bianco sono interessanti . . . dobbiamo visitarle.

4. Ha bisogno di comprare del latte?

5. Questo fiore sembra grande e bello, ma il giardino è molto piccolo.

6. Hai il tuo golf? Ho il mio e lui ha il suo.

7. Ci sono molti grandi edifici a Roma.

8. Dove sei? Sono qua . . . eccomi.

9. Preso un caffè, sono andato(a) a casa.

10. Ora ci sono pochi soldi.

11. Oggi è il primo novembre millenovecentosettantanove.

12. Partirò la seconda domenica di gennaio. Ma come sempre tornerò il prossimo mercoledì.

13. Voglio arrivarci sempre alle tre e quaranta cinque precise.

14. Quanti anni ha Giovanni? Avrà ventiquattro anni. Però secondo lui avrebbe solo vent'anni.

15. Li ha venduti a Maria. Li hai comprati tu?

16. Posso darti una mano?

17. Ho capito tutto ciò che fai.

18. Hai già bevuto la tua?
19. Ha messo i soldi in tasca.
20. L'hanno vista due volte ieri.

TRANSLATE

1. Hai capito che dobbiamo andare a casa loro?
2. Ha bisogno di un paio di scarpe.
3. Si è divertito siccome sa suonare il pianoforte.
4. Avranno venduto tutto.
5. Glielo mando.
6. Ci vedono spesso.
7. Sai chi sono loro? Sì, li conosco.
8. Si parla soltanto italiano qua.
9. Mi metto i guanti.
10. Non avremo capito la parola scritta.

ANSWERS TO REVIEW EXERCISES, TOPICS 12–16

PATTERN DRILLS

1. I ragazzi non *si alzano* puntualmente.
    I ragazzi non *si sono alzati* puntualmente.
    I ragazzi non *si saranno alzati* puntualmente.
    I ragazzi non *si sarebbero alzati* puntualmente.
2. *Dobbiamo* leggere la lista attentamente.
    Abbiamo dovuto leggere la lista attentamente.
    Avremo dovuto leggere la lista attentamente.
    Avremmo dovuto leggere la lista attentamente.
3. Chi *vuole* aiutarmi?
    Chi *ha voluto* aiutarmi?
    Chi *avrà voluto* aiutarmi?
    Chi *avrebbe voluto* aiutarmi?
4. Lei non *riesce* a spiegare l'esempio.
    Lei non *è riuscita* a spiegare l'esempio.
    Lei non *sarà riuscita* a spiegare l'esempio.
    Lei non *sarebbe riuscita* a spiegare l'esempio.
5. Io non lo *seguo*.
    Io non l'*ho seguito*.
    Io non l'*avrò seguito*.
    Io non l'*avrei seguito*.

6. Io *credo* che lui non *venga*.
   Io *credo* che lui non sia *venuto*.
7. Noi *pensiamo* che *sia* una buona idea.
   Noi *pensiamo* che *sia stata* una buona idea.
8. Loro non *sanno* se voi *abbiate capito*.
9. Questa è la più breve conferenza che io *abbia* mai *vista*.
10. Tu *vuoi* che io te ne *compri* una copia?
    Tu vuoi che io te ne *abbia comprato* una copia?
11. Io *dubito* che voi *abbiate* ragione.
    Io *dubito* che voi *abbiate avuto* ragione.
12. Benché non lo *capisca* tu, *prova* a ascoltarlo.

TRADURRE/TRANSLATION

1. Non gli piace leggere il giornale.
2. Dateci il quaderno!
3. Non dateglielo!
4. Non si sono resi conto dell'identità della ragazza.
5. Vorrebbe ritornare in Italia.
6. Lei sarà venuto troppo tardi.
7. New York è la più ricca città del mondo.
8. Ma anche Roma è una città bellissima.
9. Dino è un migliore studente di Mario, non è vero?
10. Entrando nel suo ufficio, ho veduto il quadro più piccolo e più bello del mondo.
11. Leggendo molto s'impara a pensare chiaramente.
12. Non l'hanno restituito loro.
13. Non mi scriverà?
14. Vuoi rimanere qua?
15. Ecco le bellezze della capitale d'Italia!
16. Giovanni e Maria si sono seduti presto.
17. Ho già letto il libro di cui abbiamo parlato.
18. Avrebbero fretta probabilmente.
19. Bisogna chiudere le finestre quando piove.
20. Mi sono scusato e sono uscito dalla stanza.
21. Mi hanno dato tanti problemi quante risposte.
22. Mi passi il sale e il pepe per carità.
23. Non ascoltarlo!
24. Sedetevi e abbiate pazienza!
25. Lei è più intelligente di lui.
26. Credo di poterlo fare.

SUPPLY THE CORRECT RESPONSE

1. (a) non ti abbia capito (b) molto bene
2. (a) debba pagargli (b) quello che vuole
3. (a) telefoni (b) dica
4. (a) Chi (b) due volte
5. (a) abbiano sentito ciò che
6. (a) di cui (b) lontanissimo dalla sua patria
7. (a) Bisogna (b) ricordi (c) con cui
8. (a) la cui lettera (b) vicino a noi
9. (a) A dispetto della mano che mi dà (b) da fare
10. (a) Prima di partire (b) basta
11. (a) Scrivendogliela (la lettera) (b) ne sono più contento
12. (a) seguente (b) il meglio
13. (a) Mi dia
14. (a) Aiutami (b) dammelo
15. (a) Telefonandole (b) qualche
16. (a) Per piacere, mi faccia una telefonata
17. (a) Voi chiamateli!
18. (a) Perchè sia la migliore studentessa (b) glieli
19. (a) Nata a (b) tanto (c) quanto
20. (a) avere più anni (b) di quel che
21. (a) il meglio
22. (a) delle buone OR alcune buone (b) meno (c) che
23. (a) se ne accorga
24. (a) Te (b) tu capisca
25. (a) hai capito
26. (a) piova (b) ancora voglio

ANSWERS TO REVIEW EXERCISES, TOPICS 17–20

PATTERN DRILLS

1. *Voglio* che *ci sbrighiamo.*
   Volevo che *ci sbrigassimo.*
   Vorrei che *ci sbrigassimo.*
   Avrei voluto che *ci fossimo sbrigati.*
2. Maria *pensa* che lei *debba* rispondere.
   Maria *pensava* che lei *dovesse* rispondere.
   Maria *penserebbe* che lei *dovesse* rispondere.
   Maria *avrebbe pensato* che lei *avesse dovuto* rispondere.

3. *Temo* che lui non *possa* vedere Roma.
    Temevo che lui non *potesse* vedere Roma.
    Temerei che lui non *potesse* vedere Roma.
    Avrei temuto che lui non *avesse potuto* vedere Roma.
4. *Speriamo* che loro *diano* l'indirizzo.
    Speravamo che loro *dessero* l'indirizzo.
    Spereremmo che loro *dessero* l'indirizzo.
    Avremmo sperato che loro *avessero dato* l'indirizzo.
5. Se non *nevica*, noi *andiamo* a mangiare fuori.
    Se non *nevicasse*, noi *andremmo* a mangiare fuori.
    Se non *fosse nevicato*, noi *saremmo andati* a mangiare fuori.

TRANSLATION

1. Se tornano non ci trovano.
2. Questi documenti non saranno venduti da suo nipote.
3. Vogliamo che vengano, vero?
4. Se l'insegnante non avesse spiegato la poesia, non l'avrebbe capita.
5. È appena piovuto, vero?
6. Le ragazze si sono lavate le mani.
7. Sono scontenti che gl'invitati non possano venire.
8. Non conosco nessuno che abiti qui vicino.
9. Non chiuda quella porta, per piacere.
10. Si vendono i giornali dappertutto.
11. Sebbene sia ricco, non è molto lieto.
12. Abbiamo la miglior macchina che io abbia mai vista.
13. Giovanni parla molto lentamente affinchè gli Americani lo capiscano chiaramente.
14. Sono appena andati a mangiare da Maria, ma le duole il capo (OR . . . ha un mal di testa).
15. Ho visto il libro di cui avevate parlato.
16. Come mai ti sei alzato così presto?
17. L'avevo già letto quando mi ha chiesto di comprargliene una copia.
18. Gliel'ho fatto fare.
19. Volevo che tu venissi con me. OR . . . che tu mi accompagnassi.
20. L'hanno veduta arrivare.
21. Si vendono solo i libri nuovi qua.
22. Avevo ragione! Mi vendè quella macchina cinque anni fa.
23. Sarei andato se me ne avessero detto.

24. Mentre leggevate il telefono suonò.
25. Il mio fratellino mi chiede sempre la stessa cosa.
26. Stavano per mangiare quando arrivammo.
27. Anni fa lui fece costruire una nuova camera da letto senza rendersi conto del denaro che stava spendendo.
28. Ognuno faceva come voleva.
29. Se io fossi milionario non saprei divertirmi.
30. Dopo averne letto ogni parola, io decisi di tradurre tutte le opere.

TRANSLATE THIS BRIEF TALE

When a certain poor old man decided that he could no longer stand the hunger, he took a piece of bread that he had had for a good long time and went to hold the bread over the smoke of a certain cook's fire. Angered, the cook sent him to a judge in order to pay the cook for the smoke. The sentence? The cook would be paid with the sound of a coin struck on a table.

COMPOSE. SAMPLE SENTENCES

1. Gli ho offerto un po' di pane. *I offered him a little bread.*
2. Ha rotto il bicchiere. *He broke the glass.*
3. Voglio che loro salgano prima. *I want them to go up first.*
4. Traducono la mia poesia. *They are translating my poem.*
5. Rimango a New York durante le vacanze. *I am remaining in New York during the vacation.*
6. Credo che tu abbia vinto la discussione. *I believe you won the discussion.*
7. Se scegliessero quella strada, seguirei questa. *If they chose that road, I would follow this one.*
8. Abbiamo chiuso tutte le finestre. *We have closed all the windows.*
9. Infatti, lo lesse quasi cinquanta anni fa. *As a matter of fact, he read it almost fifty years ago.*
10. Dubito che tu possa dimenticare il febbraio scorso. *I doubt you can forget last February.*

ALPHABETICAL LIST OF IRREGULAR VERBS

AVERE AND ESSERE

INFINITIVE	*AVERE*		*ESSERE*	
PRESENT PARTICIPLE	avendo		essendo	
PRESENT	ho	abbiamo	sono	siamo
	hai	avete	sei	siete
	ha	hanno	è	sono
IMPERFECT	avevo	avevamo	ero	eravamo
	avevi	avevate	eri	eravate
	aveva	avevano	era	erano
PRETERIT	ebbi	avemmo	fui	fummo
	avesti	aveste	fosti	foste
	ebbe	ebbero	fu	furono
FUTURE	avrò	avremo	sarò	saremo
	avrai	avrete	sarai	sarete
	avrà	avranno	sarà	saranno
CONDITIONAL	avrei	avremmo	sarei	saremmo
	avresti	avreste	saresti	sareste
	avrebbe	avrebbero	sarebbe	sarebbero
IMPERATIVE	—	abbiamo	—	siamo
	abbi	abbiate	sii	siate
	abbia	abbiano	sia	siano
PRESENT SUBJUNCTIVE	abbia	abbiamo	sia	siamo
	abbia	abbiate	sia	siate
	abbia	abbiano	sia	siano
IMPERFECT SUBJUNCTIVE	avessi	avessimo	fossi	fossimo
	avessi	aveste	fossi	foste
	avesse	avessero	fosse	fossero
PAST PARTICIPLE	avuto		stato, a, i, e	
PERFECT INFINITIVE	avere avuto		essere stato, a, i, e	
PLUPERFECT PARTICIPLE	avendo avuto		essendo stato, a, i, e	

PRESENT PERFECT	ho hai ha	} AVUTO	sono sei è	} STATO, A
	abbiamo avete hanno	} AVUTO	siamo siete sono	} STATI, E
FIRST PLUPERFECT	avevo avevi aveva	} AVUTO	ero eri era	} STATO, A
	avevamo avevate avevano		eravamo eravate erano	} STATI, E
SECOND PLUPERFECT	ebbi avesti ebbe	} AVUTO	fui fosti fu	} STATO, A
	avemmo aveste ebbero		fummo foste furono	} STATI, E
FUTURE PERFECT	avrò avrai avrà	} AVUTO	sarò sarai sarà	} STATO, A
	avremo avrete avranno		saremo sarete saranno	} STATI, E
CONDITIONAL PERFECT	avrei avresti avrebbe	} AVUTO	sarei saresti sarebbe	} STATO, A
	avremmo avreste avrebbero		saremmo sareste sarebbero	} STATI, E
PRESENT PERFECT SUBJUNCTIVE	abbia abbia abbia	} AVUTO	sia sia sia	} STATO, A
	abbiamo abbiate abbiano		siamo siate siano	} STATI, E
PLUPERFECT SUBJUNCTIVE	avessi avessi avesse	} AVUTO	fossi fossi fosse	} STATO, A
	avessimo aveste avessero		fossimo foste fossero	} STATI, E

INFINITIVE	*ANDARE*		*BERE*	
PRESENT PARTICIPLE	andando		bevendo	
PAST PARTICIPLE	andato		bevuto	
PRESENT	vado	andiamo	bevo	beviamo
	vai	andate	bevi	bevete
	va	vanno	beve	bevono
IMPERFECT	andavo	andavamo	bevevo	bevevamo
	andavi	andavate	bevevi	bevevate
	andava	andavano	beveva	bevevano
PRETERIT	andai	andammo	bevvi	bevemmo
	andasti	andaste	bevesti	beveste
	andò	andarono	bevve	bevvero
FUTURE	andrò	andremo	berrò	berremo
	andrai	andrete	berrai	berrete
	andrà	andranno	berrà	berranno
CONDITIONAL	andrei	andremmo	berrei	berremmo
	andresti	andreste	berresti	berreste
	andrebbe	andrebbero	berrebbe	berrebbero
IMPERATIVE	—	andiamo	—	beviamo
	va'	andate	bevi	bevete
	vada	vadano	beva	bevano
PRESENT SUBJUNCTIVE	vada	andiamo	beva	beviamo
	vada	andiate	beva	beviate
	vada	vadano	beva	bevano
IMPERFECT SUBJUNCTIVE	andassi	andassimo	bevessi	bevessimo
	andassi	andaste	bevessi	beveste
	andasse	andassero	bevesse	bevessero

INFINITIVE	*CHIUDERE*		*CONOSCERE*	
PRESENT PARTICIPLE	chiudendo		conoscendo	
PAST PARTICIPLE	chiuso		conosciuto	
PRESENT	chiudo	chiudiamo	conosco	conosciamo
	chiudi	chiudete	conosci	conoscete
	chiude	chiudono	conosce	conoscono
IMPERFECT	chiudevo	chiudevamo	conoscevo	conoscevamo
	chiudevi	chiudevate	conoscevi	conoscevate
	chiudeva	chiudevano	conosceva	conoscevano
PRETERIT	chiusi	chiudemmo	conobbi	conoscemmo
	chiudesti	chiudeste	conoscesti	conosceste
	chiuse	chiusero	conobbe	conobbero
FUTURE	chiuderò	chiuderemo	conoscerò	conosceremo
	chiuderai	chiuderete	conoscerai	conoscerete
	chiuderà	chiuderanno	conoscerà	conosceranno

CONDITIONAL	chiuderei	chiuderemmo	conoscerei	conosceremmo
	chiuderesti	chiudereste	conosceresti	conoscereste
	chiuderebbe	chiuderebbero	conoscerebbe	conoscerebbero
IMPERATIVE	—	chiudiamo	—	conosciamo
	chiudi	chiudete	conosci	conoscete
	chiuda	chiudano	conosca	conoscano
PRESENT	chiuda	chiudiamo	conosca	conosciamo
SUBJUNCTIVE	chiuda	chiudiate	conosca	conosciate
	chiuda	chiudano	conosca	conoscano
IMPERFECT	chiudessi	chiudessimo	conoscessi	conoscessimo
SUBJUNCTIVE	chiudessi	chiudeste	conoscessi	conosceste
	chiudesse	chiudessero	conoscesse	conoscessero

INFINITIVE	*DARE*		*DIRE*	
PRESENT PARTICIPLE	dando		dicendo	
PAST PARTICIPLE	dato		detto	
PRESENT	do	diamo	dico	diciamo
	dai	date	dici	dite
	dà	danno	dice	dicono
IMPERFECT	davo	davamo	dicevo	dicevamo
	davi	davate	dicevi	dicevate
	dava	davano	diceva	dicevano
PRETERIT	diedi	demmo	dissi	dicemmo
	desti	deste	dicesti	diceste
	diede	diedero	disse	dissero
FUTURE	darò	daremo	dirò	diremo
	darai	darete	dirai	direte
	darà	daranno	dirà	diranno
CONDITIONAL	darei	daremmo	direi	diremmo
	daresti	dareste	diresti	direste
	darebbe	darebbero	direbbe	direbbero
IMPERATIVE	—	diamo	—	diciamo
	da'	date	di'	dite
	dia	diano	dica	dicano
PRESENT SUBJUNCTIVE	dia	diamo	dica	diciamo
	dia	diate	dica	diciate
	dia	diano	dica	dicano
IMPERFECT SUBJUNCTIVE	dessi	dessimo	dicessi	dicessimo
	dessi	deste	dicessi	diceste
	desse	dessero	dicesse	dicessero

INFINITIVE	*DOVERE*		*FARE*	
PRESENT PARTICIPLE	dovendo		facendo	
PAST PARTICIPLE	dovuto		fatto	
PRESENT	devo	dobbiamo	faccio (fo)	facciamo
	devi	dovete	fai	fate
	deve	devono	fa	fanno
IMPERFECT	dovevo	dovevamo	facevo	facevamo
	dovevi	dovevate	facevi	facevate
	doveva	dovevano	faceva	facevano
PRETERIT	dovei	dovemmo	feci	facemmo
	dovesti	doveste	facesti	faceste
	dovè	doverono	fece	fecero
FUTURE	dovrò	dovremo	farò	faremo
	dovrai	dovrete	farai	farete
	dovrà	dovranno	farà	faranno
CONDITIONAL	dovrei	dovremmo	farei	faremmo
	dovresti	dovreste	faresti	fareste
	dovrebbe	dovrebbero	farebbe	farebbero
IMPERATIVE	—	—	—	facciamo
	—	—	fa'	fate
	—	—	faccia	facciano
PRESENT SUBJUNCTIVE	deva	dobbiamo	faccia	facciamo
	deva	dobbiate	faccia	facciate
	deva	devano	faccia	facciano
IMPERFECT SUBJUNCTIVE	dovessi	dovessimo	facessi	facessimo
	dovessi	doveste	facessi	faceste
	dovesse	dovessero	facesse	facessero

INFINITIVE	*LEGGERE*		*METTERE*	
PRESENT PARTICIPLE	leggendo		mettendo	
PAST PARTICIPLE	letto		messo	
PRESENT	leggo	leggiamo	metto	mettiamo
	leggi	leggete	metti	mettete
	legge	leggono	mette	mettono
IMPERFECT	leggevo	leggevamo	mettevo	mettevamo
	leggevi	leggevate	mettevi	mettevate
	leggeva	leggevano	metteva	mettevano
PRETERIT	lessi	leggemmo	misi	mettemmo
	leggesti	leggeste	mettesti	metteste
	lesse	lessero	mise	misero

FUTURE	leggerò	leggeremo	metterò	metteremo
	leggerai	leggerete	metterai	metterete
	leggerà	leggeranno	metterà	metteranno
CONDITIONAL	leggerei	leggeremmo	metterei	metteremmo
	leggeresti	leggereste	metteresti	mettereste
	leggerebbe	leggerebbero	metterebbe	metterebbero
IMPERATIVE	—	leggiamo	—	mettiamo
	leggi	leggete	metti	mettete
	legga	leggano	metta	mettano
PRESENT	legga	leggiamo	metta	mettiamo
SUBJUNCTIVE	legga	leggiate	metta	mettiate
	legga	leggano	metta	mettano
IMPERFECT	leggessi	leggessimo	mettessi	mettessimo
SUBJUNCTIVE	leggessi	leggeste	mettessi	metteste
	leggesse	leggessero	mettesse	mettessero

INFINITIVE	*PIACERE*		*POTERE*	
PRESENT PARTICIPLE	piacendo		potendo	
PAST PARTICIPLE	piaciuto		potuto	
PRESENT	piaccio	piacciamo	posso	possiamo
	piaci	piacete	puoi	potete
	piace	piacciono	può	possono
IMPERFECT	piacevo	piacevamo	potevo	potevamo
	piacevi	piacevate	potevi	potevate
	piaceva	piacevano	poteva	potevano
PRETERIT	piacqui	piacemmo	potei	potemmo
	piacesti	piaceste	potesti	poteste
	piacque	piacquero	potè	poterono
FUTURE	piacerò	piaceremo	potrò	potremo
	piacerai	piacerete	potrai	potrete
	piacerà	piaceranno	potrà	potranno
CONDITIONAL	piacerei	piaceremmo	potrei	potremmo
	piaceresti	piacereste	potresti	potreste
	piacerebbe	piacerebbero	potrebbe	potrebbero
IMPERATIVE	—	piacciamo	—	—
	piaci	piacete	—	—
	piaccia	piacciano	—	—
PRESENT	piaccia	piacciamo	possa	possiamo
SUBJUNCTIVE	piaccia	piacciate	possa	possiate
	piaccia	piacciano	possa	possano
IMPERFECT	piacessi	piacessimo	potessi	potessimo
SUBJUNCTIVE	piacessi	piaceste	potessi	poteste
	piacesse	piacessero	potesse	potessero

INFINITIVE	*PRENDERE*		*RISPONDERE*	
PRESENT PARTICIPLE	prendendo		rispondendo	
PAST PARTICIPLE	preso		risposto	
PRESENT	prendo	prendiamo	rispondo	rispondiamo
	prendi	prendete	rispondi	rispondete
	prende	prendono	risponde	rispondono
IMPERFECT	prendevo	prendevamo	rispondevo	rispondevamo
	predevi	predevate	rispondevi	rispondevate
	prendeva	prendevano	rispondeva	rispondevano
PRETERIT	presi	prendemmo	risposi	rispondemmo
	prendesti	prendeste	rispondesti	rispondeste
	prese	presero	rispose	risposero
FUTURE	prenderò	prenderemo	risponderò	risponderemo
	prenderai	prenderete	risponderai	risponderete
	prenderà	prenderanno	risponderà	risponderanno
CONDITIONAL	prenderei	prenderemmo	risponderei	risponderemmo
	prenderesti	prendereste	risponderesti	rispondereste
	prenderebbe	prenderebbero	risponderebbe	risponderebbero
IMPERATIVE	—	prendiamo	—	rispondiamo
	prendi	prendete	rispondi	rispondete
	prenda	prendano	risponda	rispondano
PRESENT SUBJUNCTIVE	prenda	prendiamo	risponda	rispondiamo
	prenda	prendiate	risponda	rispondiate
	prenda	prendano	risponda	rispondano
IMPERFECT SUBJUNCTIVE	prendessi	prendessimo	rispondessi	rispondessimo
	prendessi	prendeste	rispondessi	rispondeste
	prendesse	prendessero	rispondesse	rispondessero

INFINITIVE	*SALIRE*		*SAPERE*	
PRESENT PARTICIPLE	salendo		sapendo	
PAST PARTICIPLE	salito		saputo	
PRESENT	salgo	saliamo	so	sappiamo
	sali	salite	sai	sapete
	sale	salgono	sa	sanno
IMPERFECT	salivo	salivamo	sapevo	sapevamo
	salivi	salivate	sapevi	sapevate
	saliva	salivano	sapeva	sapevano
PRETERIT	salii	salimmo	seppi	sapemmo
	salisti	saliste	sapesti	sapeste
	salì	salirono	seppe	seppero

FUTURE	salirò	saliremo	saprò	sapremo
	salirai	salirete	saprai	saprete
	salirà	saliranno	saprà	sapranno
CONDITIONAL	salirei	saliremmo	saprei	sapremmo
	saliresti	salireste	sapresti	sapreste
	salirebbe	salirebbero	saprebbe	saprebbero
IMPERATIVE	—	saliamo	—	sappiamo
	sali	salite	sappi	sappiate
	salga	salgano	sappia	sappiano
PRESENT	salga	saliamo	sappia	sappiamo
SUBJUNCTIVE	salga	saliate	sappia	sappiate
	salga	salgano	sappia	sappiano
IMPERFECT	salissi	salissimo	sapessi	sapessimo
SUBJUNCTIVE	salissi	saliste	sapessi	sapeste
	salisse	salissero .	sapesse	sapessero

INFINITIVE	*SCENDERE*		*SCRIVERE*	
PRESENT PARTICIPLE	scendendo		scrivendo	
PAST PARTICIPLE	sceso		scritto	
PRESENT	scendo	scendiamo	scrivo	scriviamo
	scendi	scendete	scrivi	scrivete
	scende	scendono	scrive	scrivono
IMPERFECT	scendevo	scendevamo	scrivevo	scrivevamo
	scendevi	scendevate	scrivevi	scrivevate
	scendeva	scendevano	scriveva	scrivevano
PRETERIT	scesi	scendemmo	scrissi	scrivemmo
	scendesti	scendeste	scrivesti	scriveste
	scese	scesero	scrisse	scrissero
FUTURE	scenderò	scenderemo	scriverò	scriveremo
	scenderai	scenderete	scriverai	scriverete
	scenderà	scenderanno	scriverà	scriveranno
CONDITIONAL	scenderei	scenderemmo	scriverei	scriveremmo
	scenderesti	scendereste	scriveresti	scrivereste
	scenderebbe	scenderebbero	scriverebbe	scriverebbero
IMPERATIVE	—	scendiamo	—	scriviamo
	scendi	scendete	scrivi	scrivete
	scenda	scendano	scriva	scrivano
PRESENT	scenda	scendiamo	scriva	scriviamo
SUBJUNCTIVE	scenda	scendiate	scriva	scriviate
	scenda	scendano	scriva	scrivano
IMPERFECT	scendessi	scendessimo	scrivessi	scrivessimo
SUBJUNCTIVE	scendessi	scendeste	scrivessi	scriveste
	scendesse	scendessero	scrivesse	scrivessero

INFINITIVE	SEDERE		STARE	
PRESENT PARTICIPLE	sedendo		stando	
PAST PARTICIPLE	seduto		stato	
PRESENT	siedo	sediamo	sto	stiamo
	siedi	sedete	stai	state
	siede	siedono	sta	stanno
IMPERFECT	sedevo	sedevamo	stavo	stavamo
	sedevi	sedevate	stavi	stavate
	sedeva	sedevano	stava	stavano
PRETERIT	sedei	sedemmo	stetti	stemmo
	sedesti	sedeste	stesti	steste
	sedè	sederono	stette	stettero
FUTURE	sederò	sederemo	starò	staremo
	sederai	sederete	starai	starete
	sederà	sederanno	starà	staranno
CONDITIONAL	sederei	sederemmo	starei	staremmo
	sederesti	sedereste	staresti	stareste
	sederebbe	sederebbero	starebbe	starebbero
IMPERATIVE	—	sediamo	—	stiamo
	siedi	sedete	sta'	state
	sieda	siedano	stia	stiano
PRESENT SUBJUNCTIVE	sieda	sediamo	stia	stiamo
	sieda	sediate	stia	stiate
	sieda	siedano	stia	stiano
IMPERFECT SUBJUNCTIVE	sedessi	sedessimo	stessi	stessimo
	sedessi	sedeste	stessi	steste
	sedesse	sedessero	stesse	stessero

INFINITIVE	VEDERE		VENIRE	
PRESENT PARTICIPLE	vedendo		venendo	
PAST PARTICIPLE	veduto OR visto		venuto	
PRESENT	vedo	vediamo	vengo	veniamo
	vedi	vedete	vieni	venite
	vede	vedono	viene	vengono
IMPERFECT	vedevo	vedevamo	venivo	venivamo
	vedevi	vedevate	venivi	venivate
	vedeva	vedevano	veniva	venivano
PRETERIT	vidi	vedemmo	venni	venimmo
	vedesti	vedeste	venisti	veniste
	vide	videro	venne	vennero

FUTURE	vedrò	vedremo	verrò	verremo
	vedrai	vedrete	verrai	verrete
	vedrà	vedranno	verrà	verranno
CONDITIONAL	vedrei	vedremmo	verrei	verremmo
	vedresti	vedreste	verresti	verreste
	vedrebbe	vedrebbero	verrebbe	verrebbero
IMPERATIVE	—	vediamo	—	veniamo
	vedi	vedete	vieni	venite
	veda	vedano	venga	vengano
PRESENT SUBJUNCTIVE	veda	vediamo	venga	veniamo
	veda	vediate	venga	veniate
	veda	vedano	venga	vengano
IMPERFECT SUBJUNCTIVE	vedessi	vedessimo	venissi	venissimo
	vedessi	vedeste	venissi	veniste
	vedesse	vedessero	venisse	venissero

INFINITIVE	*VIVERE*		*VOLERE*	
PRESENT PARTICIPLE	vivendo		volendo	
PAST PARTICIPLE	vissuto		voluto	
PRESENT	vivo	viviamo	voglio	vogliamo
	vivi	vivete	vuoi	volete
	vive	vivono	vuole	vogliono
IMPERFECT	vivevo	vivevamo	volevo	volevamo
	vivevi	vivevate	volevi	volevate
	viveva	vivevano	voleva	volevano
PRETERIT	vissi	vivemmo	volli	volemmo
	vivesti	viveste	volesti	voleste
	visse	vissero	volle	vollero
FUTURE	vivrò	vivremo	vorrò	vorremo
	vivrai	vivrete	vorrai	vorrete
	vivrà	vivranno	vorrà	vorranno
CONDITIONAL	vivrei	vivremmo	vorrei	vorremmo
	vivresti	vivreste	vorresti	vorreste
	vivrebbe	vivrebbero	vorrebbe	vorrebbero
IMPERATIVE	—	viviamo	—	vogliamo
	vivi	vivete	vogli	vogliate
	viva	vivano	voglia	vogliano
PRESENT SUBJUNCTIVE	viva	viviamo	voglia	vogliamo
	viva	viviate	voglia	vogliate
	viva	vivano	voglia	vogliano
IMPERFECT SUBJUNCTIVE	vivessi	vivessimo	volessi	volessimo
	vivessi	viveste	volessi	voleste
	vivesse	vivessero	volesse	volessero

ENGLISH–ITALIAN VOCABULARY

The two vocabularies included here at the end of the review grammar are intended to provide the student with the basic word list for an effective beginning in writing, speaking, listening to, and reading the Italian language. The student should also seek to improve his or her vocabulary by noting carefully the similarity in sound and spelling of Italian words to those in English.

a uno, una
able ạbile; **to be able,** potere
about circa, quasi; **to bring about,** portare a conclusione
above sopra
absolute assoluto
accompany accompagnare
according to secondo
acquaintance conoscenza; **to make the acquaintance of,** fare la conoscenza di
across attraverso
active attivo
address indirizzo
advice consiglio
advise consigliare (di)
afraid, to be avere paura
after dopo, dopo che
afternoon pomeriggio
afterward poi
again di nuovo
against contro
age età
ago fa
ahead avanti
all tutto
almost quasi
alone solo
along lungo
aloud ad alta voce
already già

also anche
although sebbene, benchè, quantunque
always sempre
American americano
among tra
amuse divertire
and e, ed
another un altro
answer rispọndere
any alcuno, qualche, un po' di
appointment appuntamento
approach avvicinarsi
approximately circa
April aprile, m.
arm braccio (pl., le braccia)
army esẹrcito
arrive arrivare
art arte, f.
as come, da; **as for,** in quanto a
ask domandare (di), chiẹdere
asleep, to fall addormentarsi
at a, ad
attention attenzione, f.; **to pay attention,** fare caso di
August agosto
aunt zia
autumn autunno
avoid evitare (di)

baby bambino

bad cattivo
baggage bagaglio
bank banca
bath bagno; **to take a bath,** fare un
  bagno
be ẹssere, stare
beautiful bello
beauty bellezza
because perchè
bed letto
bedroom cạmera da letto
before davanti a, prima, prima che,
  avanti che
begin cominciare (a), incominciare
  (a)
believe crẹdere
bell campanello
best il migliore (adj.), il meglio
  (adv.)
better migliore (adj.), meglio (adv.)
between fra
big grande
black nero
blue azzurro
bone osso (pl. le ossa)
book libro
bookstore libreria
born nato; **to be born,** nạscere
both tutt'e due, ambedue
box scạtola
boy ragazzo
bread pane, m.
break rọmpere
breakfast colazione (f.)
bring portare
brother fratello
build costruire +
building edificio
busy occupato
but ma
butter burro
buy comprare
by da, entro

cake torta

call chiamare; **to be called,**
  chiamarsi
can potere
capital capitale, f.
car automọbile, f., mạcchina
carry portare
cash riscuọtere
cat gatto
century sẹcolo
change cambiare
Charles Carlo
charming simpạtico
check assegno
chicken pollo
choose scẹgliere
church chiesa
city città
class classe, f.
classroom aula
clean pulire +
clear chiaro
clog (n) zọccolo
close chiụdere
coffee caffè
cold freddo
color colore, m.
come venire; **come down,** scẹndere;
  come back, tornare
concerning su, a propọsito di
continue continuare (a)
cool fresco
cost costare
country campagna, paese, m.;
  pạtria
courage coraggio
cousin cugino
cover coprire
crime delitto
crowd folla
cup tazza

dance ballo; **to dance,** ballare
danger perịcolo
daughter figlia
day giorno, giornata

dear caro
death morte, f.
December dicembre, m.
delicious delizioso
departure partenza
descend scẹndere
dessert dolce, m.
die morire
different diverso
difficult diffịcile
dine pranzare
dinner pranzo
do fare
doctor mẹdico, dottore, m.
document documento
dollar dọllaro
door porta
doubt dụbbio; **to doubt,** dubitare
dressed, to get vestirsi
drink bere
during durante

each ogni, ciascuno; **each other,**
    l'un l'altro
early presto
easy fạcile
eat mangiare
egg uovo (pl., le uova)
empty vuoto
enchanting incantẹvole
end fine, f.; **to end,** finire +
English inglese
enough abbastanza; **to be enough,**
    bastare
enter entrare (in)
entrance entrata
envelope busta
especially specialmente
establish costituire +
even anche
evening sera; **good evening!** buona
    sera!; **this evening,** stasera; **in the**
    evening, sera
ever mai
every ogni

everybody tutti
everything ogni cosa
everywhere dappertutto
exact esatto; **exactly,** in punto/ap-
    punto
examination esame, m.
example esempio
except eccetto
excuse (oneself) scusarsi
exit uscita
expensive caro
explain spiegare
extreme estremo
eye occhio

fact fatto; **in fact,** infatti; **as a mat-**
    ter of fact, veramente
faith fede, f.
fall autunno (n.); cadere (v.)
family famiglia
famous famoso
far lontano
fast rạpido, veloce
father padre, m.
fear temere
feast festa
February febbraio
field campo
fight combạttere
film pellịcola
find trovare
finger dito (pl., le dita)
finish finire +
fire fuoco
first primo (adj.); prima (adv.)
fish pesce, m.; **to fish,** pescare
flower fiore, m.
fly volare
follow seguire
following seguente
foot piede, m.; **on foot,** a piedi;
    standing, in piedi
for per, da (prep.); perchè (conj.)
foreign, foreigner straniero
forget dimenticare (di)

free libero (adj.); liberare (v.)
French francese
fresco affresco
friend amico
from da
front fronte, f.; **in front of,** davanti a
fruit frutto (pl., frutta)
full pieno

garden giardino
general generale
gentleman signore, m.
German tedesco
gift regalo; **to give as a gift,** regalare
girl ragazza
give dare
glad contento
gladly volentieri
glass bicchiere, m.
glove guanto
go andare; **go down,** scendere; **go out,** uscire; **go up,** salire
God Dio
gold oro
good buono; **to have a good time,** divertirsi
goodbye addio, arrivederci, ciao
grandchild nipote, m./f.
grandfather nonno; **grandmother,** nonna
grant accordare
gray grigio
great grande
green verde
greet salutare
greeting saluto
guest invitato
guide, guidebook guida

hand mano, f.; pl., le mani
handkerchief fazzoletto
handsome bello

happen accadere
happy lieto, contento, felice
harbor porto
hard duro, difficile
hasten affrettare
hat cappello
have avere; **to have a good time,** divertirsi; **have to,** dovere
head testa; **headache** mal di testa
hear udire, sentire; **to hear about,** sentire parlare di
help aiuto; **to help,** aiutare
here qua, qui; **here is, here are,** ecco
high alto
history storia
holiday festa
home casa; **at home,** a casa
hope speranza; **to hope,** sperare (di)
horse cavallo
hot caldo
hotel albergo
hour ora
house casa; **boarding house,** pensione, f.
how come; **how much,** quanto; **how many,** quanti
however però
humanity umanità
hundred cento
hungry, to be avere fame
hurry sbrigarsi; **to be in a hurry,** avere fretta
hurt fare male a
husband marito

ice cream gelato
identity identità
if se
ill ammalato
immediately subito
important importante
improve migliorare
in in, a

ink inchiostro
instance esempio; **for instance,** per esempio
instead of invece di
intelligent intelligente
interest interessare
interesting interessante
introduce presentare
invite invitare
island isola
Italian italiano

January gennaio
John Giovanni
joke scherzo; **to joke,** scherzare
July luglio
June giugno
just giusto; **just** (with verb) appena

keep tenere
kind specie, f.; gentile
king re, m.
kitchen cucina
know conoscere, sapere

lack mancare
lady signora; **young lady,** signorina
land terra
language lingua
large grande
last durare; ultimo, scorso
late tardi (adv.), **too late,** in ritardo
laugh ridere
learn imparare
least meno; **at least,** almeno
leave partire, uscire
lecture conferenza; **to give a lecture,** fare una conferenza
left sinistro; **to the left,** a sinistra
lesson lezione, f.
letter lettera
library biblioteca
life vita
light luce, f.; leggiero

like piacere, amare; come
lip labbro (pl., le labbra)
listen (to) ascoltare
literature letteratura
little piccolo, poco; **little by little,** a poco a poco; **in a little while,** fra poco; **a little,** un poco, un po' di
live vivere, abitare
long lungo
look at guardare
look for cercare
lose perdere
loud forte
love amore, m.; amare
lunch colazione, f.; **to have lunch,** fare colazione/pranzare

madam signora
magazine rivista
magnificent magnifico
maid cameriera
mail posta; **air mail,** posta aerea; **to mail,** impostare
make fare
man uomo (pl., uomini)
March marzo
marvelous meraviglioso
Mary Maria
matter importare; **to be a matter of,** trattarsi di
May maggio
may potere
mean volere dire, significare
meat carne, f.
meet incontrare, fare la conoscenza di
midnight mezzanotte, f.
milk latte, m.
minute minuto
mirror specchio
Miss signorina
Monday lunedì, m.
money denaro, soldi
month mese, m.

more più; **more and more** sempre
    più
morning mattina; **in the morning** di
    mattina; **this morning** stamani
most il più; **at the most** al massimo
mother madre, f.
mountain monte, m., montagna
movies cinema, m.
Mr. signore, m.
Mrs. signora
much molto; **how much,** quanto; **so**
    much, tanto; **too much,** troppo
museum museo
must dovere

name nome, m.; **one's name is,**
    chiamarsi
narrow stretto
near vicino, vicino a
necessary necessario; **be necessary,**
    bisognare
necktie cravatta
need bisogno, necessita; **to have**
    need of, avere bisogno di
neither ... nor nè ... nè
nephew nipote, m.
never mai
new nuovo
newspaper giornale, m.
next venturo, prossimo
niece nipote, f.
night notte, f.; **good night,** buona
    notte; **tonight,** stasera, questa
    sera; **last night,** ieri sera, stanotte
no no; **no one,** nessuno
nobody, none nessuno
noon mezzogiorno
nor né
north nord, m.
not non; **not even,** nemmeno,
    neanche
notebook quaderno
nothing niente, nulla
notice accorgersi (di)

novel romanzo
November novembre, m.
now adesso, ora; **from now on,**
    d'ora in poi; **by now,** ormai.

object oggetto
October ottobre, m.
of di
offer offrire
office ufficio
often spesso
old vecchio, antico
on su
once una volta
one uno, una
only solo, unico (adj.); solo, sola-
    mente (adv.), soltanto (adv.)
open aprire
opening apertura
or o
order ordinare; **in order to,** per; **in**
    order that, perchè, affinchè
other altro
out fuori
owe dovere

page pagina
painted dipinto; **painting** quadro
pair paio (pl. le paia)
paper carta
pardon perdono; **to pardon,** scusare
parent genitore, m.
part parte, f.
pass passare
passenger passeggiero
past passato, scorso
patience pazienza
pay pagare; **to pay attention to,**
    fare caso di
pen penna
pencil matita
people gente, f.; popolo
pepper pepe (m.)
perfect oneself perfezionarsi

perhaps forse
person persona
physician mędico (see **doctor**)
piano pianoforte
picture quadro
place, put męttere; posto (n.),
    luogo; **to take place,** avere luogo;
    put in place, mettere a posto
plain pianura
play suonare, giocare
please per favore, per piacere, per
    carità
pleasure diletto, piacere, m.
poem poesia
poor pǫvero
porter facchino
possible possịbile
post posta; **postcard,** cartolina; **post
    office,** posta
postpone rimandare
praise lodare
pray pregare (di)
precious prezioso
prefer preferire +
present dono, regalo; **to present,**
    presentare
pretty carino, bello
prevent impedire (di) +
price prezzo
problem problema (m.)
professor professore, m.
promise promęttere
protect protęggere
proud orgoglioso
provided that purchè
pull tirare
pupil alunno
put, place męttere

quarter quarto
question domanda
quick rạpido, veloce, presto

railroad ferrovia

rain piǫvere
raincoat impermeạbile, m.
rapid rạpido
rate, at any ad ogni modo
rather piuttosto
read lęggere
reading lettura
ready pronto
real vero
realize ręndersi conto di
reason ragione, f.
receive ricęvere
recognize riconǫscere
recover guarire +
red rosso
refreshment rinfresco
relative parente, m./f.
remain rimanere
remember ricordare
repeat ripętere
require richiędere
restaurant ristorante, m.
return ritornare; restituire +
rich ricco
right diritto, destro; **to the right,** a
    destra; **to be right,** avere ragione
ring anello; **to ring,** suonare
river fiume, m.
road strada
room stanza, sala; **bathroom,**
    bagno; **bedroom,** cạmera da letto;
    dining room, sala da pranzo; **liv-
    ing room** salotto; **waiting room**
    sala d'aspetto
rose rosa
run cǫrrere

sad triste
salad insalata
salt sale (m.)
same stesso
say dire
school scuola
sea mare, m.

season stagione, f.
secret segreto
see vedere
seem parere, sembrare
sell vendere
send mandare, inviare
sentence frase, f.
separate separato; **to separate,**
 separare
September settembre, m.
serve servire
several diversi/e
sharp preciso
shirt camicia
shoe scarpa
short breve, corto; **in short,**
 insomma
shout grido; **to shout,** gridare
show spettacolo
show mostrare, fare vedere
silently silenziosamente
simple semplice
since poichè, dato che
sing cantare
sister sorella
sit down sedersi
sky cielo
sleep dormire; **to be sleepy,** avere
 sonno
slow lento
small piccolo
smart intelligente
smile sorridere
snow neve, f.; **to snow** nevicare
so così; **so much, so many,** tanto,
 tanti
some alcuno, qualche, un po' di
something qualche cosa, qualcosa
son figlio
song canzone, f.
soon presto, tra poco; **as soon as,**
 non appena; **soon after,** poco
 dopo
sorrow dolore, m.
sorry, to be dispiacere

sound suonare
soup minestra
south sud, m.
souvenir ricordo
speak parlare
special speciale
spend passare, spendere
 (for money)
spring primavera
square piazza; (n.); quadrato (adj)
stamp francobollo
start cominciare; **to start out,** partire
state stato
station stazione, f.
still ancora
stocking calza
stone pietra
stop fermarsi
store negozio
story racconto, storia
strange strano
street via
strong forte
student studente, m., studentessa
study studio; **to study** studiare
succeed succedere, riuscire (a)
suitcase valigia
summer estate, f.
Sunday domenica
supper cena
sure certo, sicuro
sweater golf
swim nuotare

table tavolo/tavola
take prendere, portare; **to take**
 place, avere luogo
tall alto
teach insegnare
teacher maestro, professore,
 insegnante
telephone telefonare; **to make a**
 telephone call, fare una telefonata

telephone telẹfono
tell dire
than che, di, di quel che
thanks grazie; to thank, ringraziare
that che, quello; that which ciò che,
    quello che
then poi, allora, dunque
there ci, là, lì; there is, there are,
    ecco; there is, c'è; there are, ci
    sono
thing cosa
think pensare
thirsty, to be avere sete
this questo
thousand mille
through per
Thursday giovedì, m.
thus così
ticket biglietto
time tempo, volta; to have a good
    time, divertirsi
timetable orario
tired stanco
to a, ad, in
today oggi
together insieme
tomorrow domani
tonight stanotte, stasera
too anche; too much, troppo; too
    many, troppi
toward verso
train treno
translation traduzione, f.
travel viaggiare
tree ạlbero
trip viaggio; to take a trip, fare un
    viaggio
true vero
truth verità
try cercare (di)
Tuesday martedì, m.
twice due volte

ugly brutto
uncle zio

under sotto
understand capire +
unforgettable indimenticạbile
unfortunately purtroppo, sfortuna-
    tamente
unhappy scontento
unite unificare, unire +
unity unità
university università
unless a meno che . . . non
until fino a, finchè
use usare
useful ụtile
useless inụtile
usually di sọlito

vacation vacanza
valise valigia
variety varietà
various diversi, -e
vengeance vendetta
very molto
view veduta
visit vịsita; to visit, visitare
voice voce, f.
voluntary volontario

wait, wait for aspettare
waiter cameriere, m.
waitress cameriera, f.
walk cammino; to walk, cammi-
    nare, passeggiare, fare una pas-
    seggiata
want volere
war guerra
warm caldo; to be warm, fare
    caldo, avere caldo
wash lavarsi; to wash dishes, lavare
    i piatti
watch orologio; to stand watch, sor-
    vegliare; to watch, guardare
weak dẹbole
wear portare
weather tempo
wedding sposalịzio

Wednesday mercoledì, m.
week settimana
welcome, benvenuto, ben tornato;
  to welcome, dare il benvenuto;
  you are welcome, prego
well bene; **very well,** benissimo; **well
  then,** dunque
what che, che cosa, quale; **that
  which,** quello che
when quando
where dove
whether se
which che, cui, quale, il quale
while mentre; **in a little while,** tra
  poco; **a little while ago,** da poco
  tempo
white bianco
who che, chi, il quale
whole tutto
why perchè, come mai
wife moglie, f. (pl., le mogli)
willing volenteroso; **willingly,** volentieri; **to be willing,** volere
win vincere
wind vento; **to be windy,** tirare vento
window finestra
wine vino

winter inverno
wise saggio
wish desiderare (di)
with con
within entro, fra, in
without senza, senza di, senza
  che
woman donna
wonderful meraviglioso
word parola
work lavoro; **to work,** lavorare
world mondo
worse peggio (adv.), peggiore (adj.)
worth valore; **to be worth,** valere
wretched misero
write scrivere
writer scrittore, m.
wrong torto; **to be wrong,** avere
  torto

year anno
yellow giallo
yes sì, già
yesterday ieri
yet ancora
young giovane; **young lady,** signorina; **young man,** giovane
youth gioventù, f., giovinezza

ITALIAN–ENGLISH VOCABULARY

a, ad at, in, to, toward
abbastanza enough
abitare to live
accomodarsi to make oneself comfortable
accompagnare to accompany
accordare to grant
accorgersi to notice
acqua water
addio good-bye
addormentarsi to fall asleep
adesso now
affannarsi (a) to strive
affare, m. business
affidare to entrust
affinchè in order that
affresco fresco
affrettare to hasten
affrontare to face
agosto August
aiutare to help
aiuto help
albergo hotel
albero tree
alcuno some, any
allora then; **d'allora in poi,** from then on
almeno at least
alto high, tall
altro other
alzare to lift
alzarsi to get up
amare to like, to love
amaro bitter
americano American
amico friend
ammalato ill
amore, m. love

analizzare analyze
anche also, too
ancora still, yet; **ancora una volta,** once more
andare to go
anno year
anticipo advance (in)
antico ancient, old
aperto open
appena just, hardly, as soon as; **appena che,** as soon as
aprile, m. April
aprire to open
ardire + to dare
armadio chest
arrabbiato angered
arrivare to arrive
arrivederci good-bye
arte, f. art
artista, m.f. artist
ascoltare to listen, to listen to
aspettare to wait, to wait for
assoluto absolute
attento attentive
attivo active, busy
attraverso across
attualmente now, at the present time
aula classroom
automobile, f. automobile
autunno autumn
avanti ahead; **avanti che,** before; **andare avanti,** to go ahead
avere to have; **avere fame,** to be hungry; **avere bisogno di,** to need; **avere fretta,** to be in a hurry; **avere luogo,** to take place; **avere paura,** to be afraid; **avere**

avere to have (*Continued*)

 ragione, to be right; **avere torto,** to be wrong

avviarsi to start out

avvicinarsi (a) to approach

azzurro blue

bagaglio baggage

bagno bath; **fare un bagno,** to take a bath

balcone balcony

ballare to dance

ballo dance

bambino baby, child

banca bank

banco bank; bench

bandiera flag

barca boat

base, f. basis, element; **a base di,** on the basis of; **in base a,** upon

basso low

bastare to be enough

battere strike

bellezza beauty

bello beautiful, handsome

benchè although

bene well

bere to drink

bianco white

biblioteca library

bicchiere, m. glass

biglietto ticket

bisognare to be necessary

bisogno need; **avere bisogno di,** to have need of

bocca mouth

bottiglia bottle

braccio arm; **le braccia,** arms

breve brief, short

brutto ugly

buono good

burro butter

busta envelope

caffè, m. coffee

caldo warm; **avere caldo,** to be warm; **fare caldo,** to be warm

calore, m. heat

calza stocking

cambiare to change; **cambiarsi,** to change clothes

camera room, esp. bedroom

cameriera waitress, maid

cameriere, m. waiter

camicia shirt

camminare to walk

campagna country, countryside

campanello bell

campo field

cane, m. dog

cantare to sing

canzone, f. song

capire + to understand

capo head

cappello hat

cappotto overcoat

carità charity

carne, f. meat

caro dear, expensive

carta paper

cartolina postcard

casa home, house

cattivo bad

cavallo horse

cena supper

cercare to look for

certamente (certo) certainly

cervello brain

che who, which, that, than; **che?** what?; **chè,** for

checchè whatever

chi who, whom; he who, he whom

chiamare to call; **chiamarsi,** to be called (named)

chiaro clear

chiedere to ask

chiesa church
chiudere to close
chiunque whoever
ci here, there
ciao good-bye
cielo sky
cinema, m. movies
cioè namely, that is
circa about, nearly
città city
classe, f. class
colazione, f. breakfast, lunch; **fare colazione,** to have breakfast, to have lunch
colore, m. color
combattere to fight
come as, like, how; **così ... come** as ... as
cominciare begin
commedia comedy
commovente touching
comodo comfortable
compagnia company
compagno companion
compleanno birthday
comprare to buy
con with
conferenza lecture; **fare una conferenza,** to give a lecture
confondersi to become confused
confuso confuso
conoscenza acquaintance; **fare la conoscenza di,** to make the acquaintance of
conoscere to know, to be acquainted with
conservare to keep
consigliare to advise
consiglio advice
consistere to consist
contento happy, glad
continuare (a) to continue
conto bill, check

contro against
copia copy
coraggio courage; **farsi coraggio,** to cheer up
correre to run
corte, f. court
corto short, brief
cosa thing
così so, thus, in brief
così ... come, as ... as; **se è così,** in that case
costare to cost
costruire + to build
cravatta necktie
creare to create
credere to believe
crudele cruel
cucina kitchen
cui which, whom
cuoco cook
cuore, m. heart

da by, from, at the house (or store) of
dappertutto everywhere
dare to give
dato che granted that
davanti a before, in front of
decidere (di) to decide
delizioso delicious
denaro money
dente, m. tooth
desiderare to wish, to desire
destare to arouse, to awaken
destro right; **a destra,** to the right
di from, of
dialogo dialogue
dicembre December
difficile difficult, hard
dimenticare (di) to forget
Dio God
dire to say, to tell
discorso speech

disinteressarsi to take no interest in
dispiacere to be sorry
distinto different, distinguished
divenire to become
diverso different; **diversi,** several, various
divertimento amusement
divertirsi to amuse oneself, to have a good time
dividere to divide
dizionario dictionary
dolce sweet
dolce, m. dessert
dolcezza sweetness
dolore, m. ache, pain, grief, sorrow
domanda question
domandare to ask (a question)
domani tomorrow
domenica Sunday
donna lady, woman
dono gift, present
dopo, dopo che after, afterwards; **poco dopo,** shortly after
dormire to sleep
dorso back
dove where
dovere must, to be obliged to, to have to
dovunque everywhere
dubbio doubt
dubitare to doubt
duomo cathedral
durante during
durare to last
duro hard

e, ed and
ecco here is, here are
edificio building
effetto effect
entrare (in) to enter
entrata entrance
entro within, by
epoca epoch

esame, m. examination
esatto exact
esercito army
esigere exact, to demand
essere to be; **essere in ritardo,** to be late
estate, f. summer
estendere to extend, to grow
estremo extreme
età age
europeo European
evitare to avoid

fa ago; **molto tempo fa,** a long time ago
faccia face
facchino porter
facile easy
fame, f. hunger; **avere fame,** to be hungry
famiglia family
famoso famous
fare to do, to make; **fare caso di,** to pay attention to; **fare colazione,** to have breakfast, to have lunch; **fare la conoscenza di,** to make the acquaintance of; **fare vedere,** to show
fatto fact
favore, m. favor; **per favore,** please
favorevole favorable
favorire + to favor
fazzoletto handkerchief
febbraio February
fede, f. faith
felice happy
fermarsi to stop
ferrovia railroad
festa feast, holiday
figlia daughter
figlio son
fine, f. end
finestra window
finire (di) + to finish

fino a until
fiore, m. flower
firmare to sign
fiume, m. river
foglio sheet
fondare to found
fondo background
fonte, f. source
forte strong, loud
forza strength
fra, among, between, in, within
francese French
francobollo stamp
frase, f. sentence
fratello brother
freddo cold; **avere freddo,** to be cold; **fare freddo,** to be cold
fresco cool; **fare fresco,** to be cool
fretta haste, hurry; **avere fretta,** to be in a hurry
frutta fruit
frutto fruit; **senza frutto,** in vain
fuggire to flee
fumo smoke
fuoco fire
fuori out, outside

gatto cat
gelato ice cream
genere, m. kind
genitore, m. parent
gennaio January
gente, f. people
gentile gentle, kind, polite
già already
giacca (giacchetta) jacket
giallo yellow
giardino garden
giocare to play; **gioco,** game
giornale, m. newspaper
giornata, giorno day
giovane young, young man
Giovanni John
giovedì Thursday

gioventù, giovinezza youth
giro tour; **fare un giro,** to make a tour
giù down
giudice judge
giugno June
golf sweater
gomma eraser
gran, grande big, large, great
gridare to shout
grido shout, scream
grigio gray
guanto glove
guardare to look, to look at
guardia policeman
guerra war
guida guide, guidebook
guidare to guide

ieri yesterday; **ieri sera,** last night
immediato immediate
imparare to learn
impermeabile, m. raincoat
importare to matter
impossibile impossible
impostare to mail
in in, into
incantevole enchanting
inchiostro ink
incominciare to begin
incontrare to meet
indietro back, backward
indimenticabile unforgettable
indirizzo address
infatti in fact
inferiore inferior
inglese English
insalata salad
insegnare to teach
insieme together
insomma in short
intanto meanwhile
intelligente intelligent
interessante interesting

interessare to interest
interesse, m. interest
interno interior, internal
inutile useless
inverno winter
inviare to send
invitare to invite
isola island
italiano Italian

là there
lago lake
largo broad
lasciare to leave, to let, to allow
latte, m. milk
lavare to wash; **lavarsi,** to wash oneself
lavorare to work
lavoro work
leggere to read
lento slow
lettera letter
letteratura literature
letto bed
lettura reading
levare to raise
lezione, f. lesson
lì there
libero free
libreria bookstore
libro book
lingua language; tongue
lira lira (money of Italy)
lodare to praise
lontano distant, far
lottare to fight, to struggle
luglio July
lume, m. light
luna moon
lunedì, m. Monday
lungo long
luogo place; **avere luogo,** to take place

ma but
macchina machine; **macchina da scrivere,** typewriter
madre, f. mother
maestro teacher
magazzino stock, store
maggio May
maggiore greater, greatest; older, oldest
magnifico magnificent
mai ever, never
male bad; **male,** m. evil
malgrado in spite of
malvagio wicked
mancanza lack
mancare to lack
mandare to send
mangiare to eat
mano, f. hand; **a larga mano,** generously; **dare una mano a,** to help
mare, m. sea
marinare skip (class)
martedì, m. Tuesday
marzo March
massimo very great; **al massimo,** at the most
matita pencil
mattina morning; **di mattina,** in the morning
medico physician (doctor)
meglio better (adv.)
menare to lead
meno less; **a meno che non,** unless
mensa table
mente, f. mind
mentre while
meraviglioso marvelous
mercoledì, m. Wednesday
mese, m. month
mettere to place, to put
mezzanotte, f. midnight
mezzo half; **mezzo,** n. means

mezzogiorno noon
migliorare to better, to improve
migliore better, best (adj.)
minuto minuto
mirare to look at
misero miserable, wretched
modo manner; **ad ogni modo**, at any rate; **in tal modo**, thus
moglie, f. wife
molto many, much, very
momento moment
mondo world
moneta coin, money
monte, m. mountain
morire to die
morte, f. death
mostrare to show
muovere to move
muro wall
museo museum
mutare to change
muto silent

nascere to be born
naturale natural
nè ... nè neither ... nor
ne some, any
neanche not even
necessario necessary
negare to deny
negozio shop, store
nemmeno not even
nero black
nessuno no one, nobody
neve, f. snow
nevicare to snow
niente nothing
nipote, m./f. nephew, niece
no no
nome, m. name
non not
notare to notice
novembre, m. November

nulla nothing
numero number
nuotare to swim
nuovo new; **di nuovo**, again

o or
obbligare to oblige
occhio eye
offrire (di) to offer
oggetto object
oggi today
ogni each, every
onesto honest, fair
opporre to oppose
ora now; hour
orario timetable
ordinare (di) to order
ordine, m. order
orgoglio pride
orgoglioso proud
oro gold
osare to dare
osservare to observe
ottenere to obtain
ottobre, m. October

pacco package
padre, m. father
paese, m. country
pagare to pay
paio pair
pane, m. bread
papa, m. pope
parente, m./f. relative
parere to appear, to seem
parlare to speak, to talk
parola word
parte, f. part, side; **da ogni parte**, from everywhere; **da parte mia**, on my behalf
partenza departure
partire to depart, to leave
passare to pass, to spend

passeggiare to take a walk
passeggiata walk; **fare una passeggiata,** to take a walk
passeggiero passenger
patire + to suffer
patria country
paura fear; **avere paura,** to be afraid
pazzo crazy
pellicola film
penna pen
pensare to think
pepe pepper
per by, for, through, in order to; **per quanto,** however
perchè because, why, in order that
perdere to lose
pericoloso dangerous
periglio danger
però however
persona person
pesce, m. fish
pezzo piece
piacere, m. pleasure; **piacere,** to be pleasing, to please
piazza square
piccolo little, small
piede, m. foot; **a piedi,** on foot
pieno full
pietà pity
pietra stone
piovere to rain
più more
piuttosto rather
poco (po') little; **a poco a poco,** little by little
poesia poetry
poeta poet (m.)
poi then
poichè since
pollo chicken
pomeriggio afternoon
ponte, m. bridge
popolare popular

popolo people
porco pig
porta door
portare to bring; to wear
posare to set down
posta mail, post office
posto place
potere can, to be able
povero poor
pranzare to dine
pranzo dinner
preciso sharp, exactly
preferire + to prefer
pregare to pray
prendere to take
presentare to introduce, to present
prestare to lend
presto early, quickly, quick
prezioso precious
prezzo price
prima before, first
primavera spring
primo first
principe prince
principiare to begin, to start
probabile probable
problema, m. problem
professore, m. professor
pronto ready
proseguire to continue
provare to prove; to find out
pulire + to clean
punto point; **punto di vista,** point of view; **puntualmente,** punctually
purchè provided that
pure also, yet
purtroppo unfortunately

qua here
quaderno notebook
quadrato square (adj.)
qualche any, some
quale what, which; **il quale,** who, whom, which, that

quando when
quanto how many, how much
quantunque although
quasi almost
quello that
questo this
qui here

ragazza girl
ragazzo boy
ragione, f. reason; **avere ragione,** to be right
rapido fast, rapid
rappresentare to represent
regalo gift, present
rendersi conto di to realize
restare to remain
ricco rich
ricevere to receive
richiedere to require
riconoscere to recognize
ricordare (di) to remember
ridare to give back, to return
ridere to laugh
riferirsi + to refer
rimandare to postpone
rimanere to remain
ripetere to repeat
riposarsi to take a rest
rispondere to answer
ristorante, m. restaurant
ritardo delay; **essere in ritardo,** to be late; **in ritardo,** too late
ritornare to be late
riuscire (a) to succeed
rivedere to see again
rivista magazine
romanzo novel
rosso red

sabato Saturday
sala hall, room; **sala da pranzo,** dining room; **sala d'aspetto,** waiting room

salire to go up, to climb
salutare to greet
saluto greeting
sapere to know
sbagliare to be mistaken
sbaglio mistake
sbrigarsi to hurry
scarpa shoe
scendere to descend, to go down
scherzare to joke
scherzo joke
scontento unhappy
scordarsi to forget
scorso last
scrivere to write
scuola school
scusarsi to excuse oneself
se if, whether
sebbene although
secolo century
secondo according to, second
sedersi to sit down
segreto secret
seguente following
seguire (a) to follow
sembrare to appear, to seem
sempre always
sentire to feel, to hear
senza, senza che without
sera evening
servire to serve
settembre, m. September
sete, f. thirst; **avere sete,** to be thirsty
settimana week
sì yes
sicuro safe, sure
significare to mean
signora lady, woman, Mrs.
signore, m. gentleman, sir, Mr.
signorina young lady, Miss
simpatia sympathy, liking
simpatico nice, pleasant
sinistro left; **a sinistra,** to the left

slancio rush, impulse
soccorrere to help
sognare to dream
sogno dream
solamente only
sole, m. sun
solito usual; **di solito,** usually; **al solito,** as usual
solo alone, only
soltanto only
sommare to add
sonno sleep; **avere sonno,** to be sleepy
sopportare stand, endure
sorella sister
sorridere to smile
sotto under
spazio space
specie, f. kind
speranza hope
sperare (di) to hope
spesso often
spiegare to explain
sportello door, (cage) window
sposalizio wedding
squisito exquisite
stabilirsi + to settle down
stagione, f. season
stamani this morning
stanco tired
stanotte last night, tonight
stanza room
stare to be; **stare per,** to be about to
stasera this evening, tonight
stato state
stazione, f. station
stesso same
storia history, story
storico historic/historian
strada road, street
straniero foreign; foreigner, stranger
stretto close, narrow

studente, m. student
studentessa, f. student
studiare to study
studioso studious/scholar
su on, upon
subito at once, immediately
suonare to ring, to sound, to play
suono sound
Svizzera Switzerland
svizzera, Swiss

tagliare to cut
tale such
tanto so much, so many; **tanto . . . quanto,** as . . . as
tardi late (adv.)
tassi, m. taxi
tavolo table
tazza cup
tedesco German
telefonare to telephone
telefonata telephone call; **fare una telefonata,** to make a telephone call.
telefono telephone
temere (di) to fear
tempo time, weather
tenere to have, to hold
tentare to attempt
terra earth, ground
tirare to pull
tornare (a) to return
torto wrong; **avere torte,** to be wrong
traduzione, f. translation
trattarsi di to be a question of
traversare to cross
treno train
triste sad
troppo too, too many, too much
trovare to find; **trovarsi,** to be situated
turista, m./f. tourist
tutto all; **tutti,** everyone

udire to hear
ufficio office
ultimo last
umanità humanity
uno, una a, an; one
unico only
unire + to join, to unite
università university
uomo man: uomini, men
uovo egg: le uova, eggs
usanza custom
usare to use
usciere, m. usher
uscire to go out
uscita exit
utile useful

vacanza vacation
valere to be worth
valigia valise, suitcase
valle, f. valley
vantaggio advantage
vantaggioso advantageous
vecchio old
vedere to see
veduta sight, view
veloce fast
vendere to sell
venerdì, m. Friday
venire to come
vento wind; tirare vento, to be
 windy
verde green

vero true
verità truth
verso toward; verse
vestirsi to get dressed
via street
viaggiare to travel
viaggio trip; fare un viaggio, to take
 a trip
vicino neighboring; vicino a,
 near
vino wine
virtù, f. virtue
visita visit
visitare to visit
vita life
vivere to live
voce, f. voice; ad alta voce, in a
 loud voice
voglia desire
volare to fly
volentieri gladly, willingly
volere to want, to wish, to be willing; volere dire, to mean
volgersi to turn
volo flight
volta time, turn; ancora una volta,
 once more; una volta, once
vuoto empty

zia aunt
zio uncle
zoccolo clog
zucchero sugar

INDEX